BARBARA JORDAN

BARBARA JORDAN

Rose Blue and Corinne Naden

Senior Consulting Editor
Nathan Irvin Huggins
Director
W.E.B. Du Bois Institute for Afro-American Research
Harvard University

CHELSEA HOUSE PUBLISHERS
Philadelphia

$22.95

Chelsea House Publishers

Editor-in-Chief Remmel Nunn
Managing Editor Karyn Gullen Browne
Copy Chief Mark Rifkin
Picture Editor Adrian G. Allen
Art Director Maria Epes
Assistant Art Director Howard Brotman
Manufacturing Director Gerald Levine
Systems Manager Lindsey Ottman
Production Manager Joseph Romano
Production Coordinator Marie Claire Cebrián

Black Americans of Achievement
Senior Editor Richard Rennert

Staff for BARBARA JORDAN
Text Editor Marian W. Taylor
Copy Editor Christopher Duffy
Editorial Assistant Michele Berezansky
Designer Ghila Krajzman
Picture Researcher Joan Beard
Cover Illustration Daniel Mark Duffy

7 9 8

Library of Congress Cataloging-in-Publication Data

Naden, Corinne J.
   Barbara Jordan: politician/by Corinne Naden and Rose Blue.
   p. cm.—(Black Americans of achievement)
   Includes bibliographical references and index.
   ISBN   0-7910-1131-3
         0-7910-1156-9 (pbk.)
   1. Jordan, Barbara, 1936—Juvenile literature. 2. Legislators—United
States—Biography—Juvenile literature. 3.United States. Congress.
House—Biography—Juvenile literature. [1. Jordan, Barbara, 1936– .
2. Legislators. 3. Afro-Americans—Biography] I. Blue, Rose. I. Title.
II. Series.
E840.8.J62M33 1991   91-24410
[B]   CIP
328.73'092—dc20   AC

Frontispiece: *Congresswoman
Barbara Jordan of Texas, keynote
speaker at the 1976 Democratic
National Convention, signs an
autograph at New York City's
Madison Square Garden.*

CONTENTS

BLACK AMERICANS OF ACHIEVEMENT

HENRY AARON
baseball great

KAREEM ABDUL-JABBAR
basketball great

MUHAMMAD ALI
heavyweight champion

RICHARD ALLEN
*religious leader and
social activist*

MAYA ANGELOU
author

LOUIS ARMSTRONG
musician

ARTHUR ASHE
tennis great

JOSEPHINE BAKER
entertainer

JAMES BALDWIN
author

TYRA BANKS
model

BENJAMIN BANNEKER
scientist and mathematician

COUNT BASIE
bandleader and composer

ROMARE BEARDEN
artist

JAMES BECKWOURTH
frontiersman

MARY MCLEOD BETHUNE
educator

GEORGE WASHINGTON
CARVER
botanist

BILL COSBY
entertainer

PAUL CUFFE
merchant and abolitionist

MILES DAVIS
musician

FREDERICK DOUGLASS
abolitionist

CHARLES DREW
physician

W. E. B. DU BOIS
scholar and activist

PAUL LAURENCE DUNBAR
poet

DUKE ELLINGTON
bandleader and composer

RALPH ELLISON
author

JULIUS ERVING
basketball great

LOUIS FARRAKHAN
political activist

ELLA FITZGERALD
singer

MORGAN FREEMAN
actor

MARCUS GARVEY
black nationalist leader

JOSH GIBSON
baseball great

DIZZY GILLESPIE
musician

WHOOPI GOLDBERG
entertainer

ALEX HALEY
author

PRINCE HALL
social reformer

JIMI HENDRIX
musician

MATTHEW HENSON
explorer

GREGORY HINES
performer

BILLIE HOLIDAY
singer

LENA HORNE
entertainer

WHITNEY HOUSTON
singer and actress

LANGSTON HUGHES
poet

ZORA NEALE HURSTON
author

JESSE JACKSON
civil-rights leader and politician

MICHAEL JACKSON
entertainer

JACK JOHNSON
heavyweight champion

MAGIC JOHNSON
basketball great

SCOTT JOPLIN
composer

BARBARA JORDAN
politician

MICHAEL JORDAN
basketball great

CORETTA SCOTT KING
civil-rights leader

MARTIN LUTHER KING, JR.
civil-rights leader

LEWIS LATIMER
scientist

SPIKE LEE
filmmaker

CARL LEWIS
champion athlete

JOE LOUIS
heavyweight champion

RONALD MCNAIR
astronaut

MALCOLM X
militant black leader

BOB MARLEY
musician

THURGOOD MARSHALL
Supreme Court justice

TONI MORRISON
author

ELIJAH MUHAMMAD
religious leader

EDDIE MURPHY
entertainer

JESSE OWENS
champion athlete

SATCHEL PAIGE
baseball great

CHARLIE PARKER
musician

ROSA PARKS
civil-rights leader

SIDNEY POITIER
actor

ADAM CLAYTON POWELL,
JR.
political leader

COLIN POWELL
military leader

A. PHILIP RANDOLPH
labor leader

PAUL ROBESON
singer and actor

JACKIE ROBINSON
baseball great

DIANA ROSS
entertainer

WILL SMITH
actor

CLARENCE THOMAS
Supreme Court justice

SOJOURNER TRUTH
antislavery activist

HARRIET TUBMAN
antislavery activist

NAT TURNER
slave revolt leader

TINA TURNER
singer

ALICE WALKER
author

MADAM C. J. WALKER
entrepreneur

BOOKER T. WASHINGTON
educator

DENZEL WASHINGTON
actor

VANESSA L. WILLIAMS
singer and actress

OPRAH WINFREY
entertainer

TIGER WOODS
golf star

RICHARD WRIGHT
author

ON
ACHIEVEMENT

———— ❧ ————

Coretta Scott King

BEFORE YOU BEGIN this book, I hope you will ask yourself what the word *excellence* means to you. I think that it's a question we should all ask, and keep asking as we grow older and change. Because the truest answer to it should never change. When you think of excellence, perhaps you think of success at work; or of becoming wealthy; or meeting the right person, getting married, and having a good family life.

Those important goals are worth striving for, but there is a better way to look at excellence. As Martin Luther King, Jr., said in one of his last sermons, "I want you to be first in love. I want you to be first in moral excellence. I want you to be first in generosity. If you want to be important, wonderful. If you want to be great, wonderful. But recognize that he who is greatest among you shall be your servant."

My husband, Martin Luther King, Jr., knew that the true meaning of achievement is service. When I met him, in 1952, he was already ordained as a Baptist preacher and was working toward a doctoral degree at Boston University. I was studying at the New England Conservatory and dreamed of accomplishments in music. We married a year later, and after I graduated the following year we moved to Montgomery, Alabama. We didn't know it then, but our notions of achievement were about to undergo a dramatic change.

You may have read or heard about what happened next. What began with the boycott of a local bus line grew into a national movement, and by the time he was assassinated in 1968 my husband had fashioned a black movement powerful enough to shatter forever the practice of racial segregation. What you may not have read about is where he got his method for resisting injustice without compromising his religious beliefs.

He adopted the strategy of nonviolence from a man of a different race, who lived in a different country, and even practiced a different religion. The man was Mahatma Gandhi, the great leader of India, who devoted his life to serving humanity in the spirit of love and nonviolence. It was in these principles that Martin discovered his method for social reform. More than anything else, those two principles were the key to his achievements.

This book is about black Americans who served society through the excellence of their achievements. It forms a part of the rich history of black men and women in America—a history of stunning accomplishments in every field of human endeavor, from literature and art to science, industry, education, diplomacy, athletics, jurisprudence, even polar exploration.

Not all of the people in this history had the same ideals, but I think you will find something that all of them had in common. Like Martin Luther King, Jr., they all decided to become "drum majors" and serve humanity. In that principle—whether it was expressed in books, inventions, or song—they found something outside themselves to use as a goal and a guide. Something that showed them a way to serve others, instead of only living for themselves.

Reading the stories of these courageous men and women not only helps us discover the principles that we will use to guide our own lives but also teaches us about our black heritage and about America itself. It is crucial for us to know the heroes and heroines of our history and to realize that the price we paid in our struggle for equality in America was dear. But we must also understand that we have gotten as far as we have partly because America's democratic system and ideals made it possible.

We are still struggling with racism and prejudice. But the great men and women in this series are a tribute to the spirit of our democratic ideals and the system in which they have flourished. And that makes their stories special and worth knowing. ❧

"I, BARBARA JORDAN . . ."

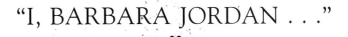

THE DAY OF July 12, 1976, was a scorcher, especially in densely packed, heat-retaining New York City. Air conditioners rumbled nonstop, soft drink vendors grew rich, and wilting pedestrians barely crawled. Even the usually hyperactive pigeons seemed listless.

But in Madison Square Garden, nobody seemed to care about the heat. The hordes of people who jammed the vast arena appeared, in fact, to be having the time of their life. Straw hatted and festooned with pins and badges, they paraded exuberantly through the aisles, talking, shouting, singing, and waving banners.

The merrymakers were delegates, representing all 50 states and the U.S. territories, to the 1976 Democratic National Convention. Every four years, each of America's political parties holds such an assembly, convened to nominate candidates for president and vice-president of the United States.

The Democrats were unusually excited about this convention. Not until the following month, when they convened in Kansas City, Missouri, would the

Barbara Jordan acknowledges a roar of applause following her keynote speech at the 1976 Democratic National Convention. After the electrifying address, one newspaper observed that the Democrats "never had an opening night like this before, and never will again."

Senator John Glenn of Ohio, whose keynote lecture preceded Jordan's, takes the podium at the 1976 convention. Despite his fame and popularity, former astronaut Glenn failed to capture the interest of delegates, who kept up a steady stream of chatter during his speech.

Republicans officially select their choices to run in the November election. Nevertheless, everyone at the Garden knew their opponents would name the current president, Gerald Ford, to carry the Republican standard. And this delighted the Democrats.

They were confident that this time, after two disastrous elections, they could recapture the White House. The Republicans had controlled it since 1968, when former vice-president Richard M. Nixon trounced Senator Hubert H. Humphrey of Minnesota. In 1972, Nixon had won a second term, easily defeating Senator George S. McGovern of South Dakota.

In 1973, Nixon's vice-president, Spiro Agnew, resigned after admitting to tax evasion; as his replacement, Nixon nominated and Congress confirmed Gerald Ford, Republican leader of the House of Representatives. One year later, a political scandal known as Watergate forced Nixon to resign from office, making him the first U.S. president to do so.

Ford then became president, the first to serve without being chosen in a national election.

A month after he took office, Ford pardoned Nixon for any federal crimes he might have committed, including those connected with the Watergate affair. The Democrats believed that the pardon, unpopular with the American people, could cost Ford the 1976 election—a belief that explained the jubilant mood at the 1976 convention.

As Americans watched the action at the Garden on television, they must have wondered how this unruly mob could accomplish anything, let alone select a presidential candidate. No one at the convention seemed to be paying attention to anyone else—not to the delegation leaders, not to the harassed people trying to make announcements over the public address system, not to the various politicians droning on from the platform.

National political conventions always feature a keynote speaker, an individual whose words are expected to prove the occasion's high point. Ideally, the keynote speech sets the tone, points the way, spells out the party's ideals and hopes for the nation. This convention would boast not one but two carefully selected keynoters.

The first was a white male, Senator John Glenn of Ohio. A former astronaut, Glenn had gained instant celebrity in 1962, when he became the first American to orbit the earth. The second keynoter was a black female, Barbara Jordan of Texas. A member of the U.S. House of Representatives, Jordan had been the first black woman elected to represent any state of the Deep South.

Sure that he had picked an unbeatable combination, Democratic National Committee chairman Robert Strauss had particularly counted on Glenn. But as he listened to the popular legislator speak, Strauss's heart sank. Colorless and uninspired,

Glenn's lecture grew duller by the minute, failing to stop or even slow down the chatter among the delegates.

Even before Glenn's speech, Strauss had been having problems. Envisioning a convention united in cheers for his biracial, two-gender team, he had earlier tried to persuade Jordan to walk to the podium with Glenn. Jordan, who had a bad knee due to damaged cartilage, had vetoed that idea.

To make matters worse, Jordan had shown signs of nervousness. Strauss assured the handsome congresswoman—resplendent in a light green three-piece suit and newly svelte after a recent diet—that she had nothing to worry about. He told her to concentrate on the 75 million television viewers at home. "Don't pay any attention to the people in the Garden," he said. "They won't be paying attention to you."

Strauss is famous for his political savvy, but this time he was dead wrong. As Jordan began to speak, the crowd seemed to sense that something quite

Flanking 1976 Democratic presidential candidate Jimmy Carter (center) are (from left to right) his mother, Lillian; his daughter, Amy; and his wife, Rosalynn. At right are the vice-presidential candidate, Senator Walter Mondale of Minnesota, and his wife, Joan. Some political observers believed that Mondale's spot might have gone to Jordan had she and Carter not both hailed from the Deep South.

extraordinary was happening. Probably no one actually said, "Hey, this is historic—quiet down and listen!" but the crowd was soon silent. Vibrating with strength and conviction, Jordan's sonorous voice rang out, filling every corner of the crowded, smoky arena. All eyes turned to the podium and the tall, commanding woman who was saying:

> One hundred and forty-four years ago, members of the Democratic party first met in convention to select a presidential candidate. Since that time, Democrats have continued to convene once every four years and draft a party platform and nominate a presidential candidate. And our meeting this week is a continuation of that tradition.

> But there is something different about tonight. There is something special about tonight. What is different? What is special? *I, Barbara Jordan*, am a keynote speaker.

As she continued, the cavernous auditorium became almost eerily silent. No one moved; no one talked. They listened. Jordan later remembered losing her jitters and thinking, "This is the way it will be." Throughout her address, she held the packed Garden and the audience at home in the palm of her hand. In resonant tones, she went on:

> A lot of years [have] passed since 1832 [the date of the first Democratic party convention], and during that time it would have been most unusual for any national political party to ask that a Barbara Jordan deliver a keynote address . . . but tonight here I am. And I feel, notwithstanding the past, that my presence here is one additional bit of evidence that the American Dream need not forever be deferred.

Winding up, she said:

> Now, I began this speech by commenting to you on the uniqueness of a Barbara Jordan making the keynote address. Well, I am going to close my speech by quoting a Republican president, and I ask that as you listen to these words of Abraham Lincoln, you relate them to the concept of a national community in which every last one of us participates: "As I would not be a *slave*, so I would not be a *master*. This expresses my idea of democracy. Whatever

differs from this, to the extent of the difference, is no democracy."

When Jordan finished, the crowd went wild. One awestruck woman approached the congresswoman and said, "If God is a woman, she must sound like you." Delegates began to chant, "We want Barbara!" Strauss was exultant. "I told them she'd be the hit of the show!" he shouted. The next day's newspapers agreed.

"A classic American success story," proclaimed the *New York Times*. "They jumped and cheered and clapped and stomped and yelled—and loved her," proudly declared the *Houston Post* of Jordan's home state. "The Democrats were losing to boredom, 1–0, last night when they had the good sense to bring Barbara Jordan off the bench," observed Philadelphia's *Evening Bulletin*. "The Democratic party, which has been at this convention business for 144 years, never had an opening night like this before," concluded the *Washington Star*, "and never will again."

Had Jordan not hailed from the Deep South, some political observers noted, her speech might even have earned her the vice-presidential nomination. But the Democrats' presidential candidate was Jimmy Carter of Georgia, and unwritten American political law decrees that a party's two top candidates must be from different sections of the country. Nevertheless, that speech catapulted Jordan to center stage in the nation's political theater. As a fellow representative said of her after the keynote speech, "We sent the best we had."

By the time of the 1976 convention, 40-year-old Barbara Jordan had already made a name for herself. Other Democrats, members of Congress, and a large part of the American public recognized her as both brilliant and hardworking. Jordan had made her first official political speech on March 15, 1967, two

months after her election to the Texas State Senate. One long-term legislator called that address "the finest maiden speech ever made by a Texas senator."

The freshman senator had taken the floor to attack a proposed increase in Houston's city sales tax. "Forty percent of the people of this state make under $3,000 a year, which the federal government has designated as the poverty level," she said, her voice rising steadily. "Where is the equity in a situation where the people who earn the most pay the least tax, and those who earn the least pay the most?" In the end, Jordan lost her fight against the tax bill, but she had been heard, and she was remembered.

Other impressive Jordan speeches, each displaying decisive knowledge of her subject, had followed; she became known as a legislator who did her homework. In 1972, she won election to the U.S. House of Representatives and began to gain national prominence.

Almost bowled over by cheers, whistles, foot stamping, and hand clapping after her convention speech, Jordan laughs helplessly as Democratic National Committee chairman Robert Strauss tries to silence the crowd.

In Congress, Jordan became a member of the House Judiciary Committee, which at that point was considering the Watergate scandal and the possible impeachment (charge of misconduct in office) of President Nixon. Watergate began with agents of Nixon's reelection committee breaking into Democratic party headquarters in Washington, D.C.'s Watergate building.

Discovery of the break-in had triggered a political earthquake and thrown light on a dark, tangled web of conspiracies and illegal secret dealings by high government officials, including the president. It was the assignment of the Judiciary Committee to determine the extent of Nixon's illegal involvement in the Watergate affair.

Jordan agonized over the question of impeachment. "I have the same high regard for the office of the president as the majority of Americans," she said. And she had the same high regard for the laws of the land. During the Watergate investigation, the Judiciary Committee demanded that the Nixon administration turn over a series of tapes that had been recorded in the White House after the break-in and subsequent cover-up.

When the administration finally surrendered the tapes, they had been deliberately falsified—laced with gaps or humming sounds instead of words. The tactic outraged Jordan. "There are no gaps, there are no inexplicable 'hums,'" she snapped, "in the Constitution of the United States."

The idea of elected officials betraying public trust and constitutional ideals obviously infuriated Jordan, who made no secret of her beliefs. When the Judiciary Committee began its televised debate on the impeachment in July 1974, her passionate convictions gained her more national attention. "My faith in the Constitution is whole, it is complete, it is total," she thundered at one point. "I am not going to sit here and be an idle spectator to the diminution, the subversion, the destruction, of the Constitution!"

Barbara Charline Jordan, American female, black, intellectual, politician, college professor, was in some ways a paradox. She commanded respect— and even awe—for the strength of her convictions and the quality of her mind, and millions were stirred by her ringing statements and rich voice. Yet she was called aloof, even cold, a solitary figure going her own way, marching to her own drummer. Jordan was an extremely private woman, but what she revealed about her life makes a fascinating story.

It begins in her home state of Texas, in the city of Houston.

2

SEPARATE BUT EQUAL?

Barbara Jordan—whose cheery smile and frank gaze would remain virtually unchanged as the years passed—decided to join the Baptist church when she was 10. "I got tired of being a sinner," she said.

BARBARA CHARLINE JORDAN was born on February 21, 1936, in Houston, Texas. The third child of Arlyne Jordan and her husband, Benjamin, Barbara had two older sisters, Rose Mary and Bennie.

The Jordan girls spent their early years in a pink-trimmed brick home in the Fifth Ward, one of the few black districts in Houston that boasted tall trees, paved streets, electricity, and residences with indoor plumbing. Sharing the two-bedroom house with the five Jordans were Benjamin Jordan's father, Charles, a truck driver and church deacon, and Charles's second wife, Alice, a high school English teacher. The parents and grandparents had their own rooms; the girls shared a fold-out bed in the dining room.

Closer to young Barbara than these relatives was her mother's father, John Ed Patten. A fiercely independent man who operated a junkyard, he adored his youngest granddaughter. She spent every Sunday with him, helping to sort the rags, scrap metal, and old newspapers that he collected and sold. "My grandfather always gave me part of the money," she recalled later. "We got on famously."

Grandfather Patten was the only man in Barbara's family who did not attend church. He often read to

Barbara's grandfather, John Ed Patten, called her My Heart and tried to teach her the philosophy that had sustained him in a difficult life. The most important mission of experience, he told her, was "to teach us how better we should love."

her from the Bible, however, and he decorated his property with such messages as The Lord Is My Shepherd and The Day of Wrath Is Come. He also gave his favorite granddaughter copious advice, much of which related to independence. "You just trot your own horse and don't get into the same rut as everyone else," he told her.

Patten had a favorite maxim, which Barbara memorized and which she quoted in her 1979 autobiography, *Barbara Jordan: A Self-Portrait:* "Just remember the world is not a playground, but a schoolroom. Life is not a holiday but an education.

One eternal lesson for us all: to teach us how better we should love." That, said the adult Jordan, "was a very nice sentiment."

John Ed Patten had known more than his share of trouble: Crooked suppliers had swindled him out of a candy store he had once owned, and years before Barbara's birth he had served seven years in jail for shooting at—but not hitting—a white police officer he had mistaken for a thief. Despite his problems, the old man seemed serene and happy to Barbara. "Look, this man can make it, my grandfather," she said to herself. "He can put together whatever combination of things necessary and just kind of make it." Thinking about it years later, she said, "And that had an impact on me."

Patten had nurtured high hopes for his daughter Arlyne, Barbara's mother. As a young woman, Arlyne earned widespread praise as an orator at local Baptist conventions. "She was the most eloquent, articulate person I ever heard; if she'd been a man she would have been a preacher," recalled one impressed churchgoer. Arlyne's proud father encouraged her, helping her expand her vocabulary and acting as her speech coach.

Then, barely out of high school, Arlyne met and married Ben Jordan, a handsome student at Alabama's Tuskegee Institute, the college founded by prominent black leader Booker T. Washington in 1881. Arlyne's father was furious. He refused to attend her wedding and, as he watched her wait on her husband and spend her days cooking and cleaning, grew increasingly estranged.

But when Barbara (delivered by her mother's cousin, Dr. Thelma Patten) was born, John Patten felt a new surge of hope and love. He even began carrying a photograph of the baby, inscribed My Heart. "Here at last was someone to whom he could give all the lessons he had learned," wrote the adult

Barbara. "He gave her a God who did not say bend your knee and await a better day. He gave her autonomy, telling her, 'Do not take a boss. Do not marry. Look at your mother.'" John Patten's granddaughter never forgot his words.

All the Jordans were devout Baptists. Like her sisters, Barbara began attending church services before she could walk or talk; by the time she was 10, she had decided she was "tired of being a sinner" and joined the church as a full-fledged member. Ben Jordan watched with pride as his little girl "took the right hand of fellowship" in the Good Hope Missionary Baptist Church. Two years later, in 1947, he rose to his feet in the same church and announced that he had been "called to preach."

In 1949, when Barbara was 13, her father took on the full-time work of a minister in addition to his job at the Houston Terminal Warehouse and Cold Storage Company. At the same time, he moved his family out of his father's house and into their own home on Campbell Street. The new place was in one of Houston's poorest black neighborhoods, but the Jordans took great pride in it: Their neat wooden house was always crisply painted (in pink, the family's favorite color); its yard, trimly mowed. Ben Jordan set high standards both for himself and his family.

Jordan was a stern, exacting father. "He never struck us," recalled his oldest daughter, Rose Mary, "but the way he talked to us when he was displeased was more of a punishment than Mother's spankings. Just to have him question you frightened you to the point of never doing it again." The Jordan girls were allowed what Rose Mary called "limited recreational activities"; they were permitted to play with the other neighborhood children on summer evenings, she said, but only "till we were called in at curfew."

The Jordans taught their daughters to carry themselves with dignity, to value education and hard work, and to respect their elders. Barbara Jordan, who has been credited with exceptional self-control, has said she owes it to her father. She was absolutely forbidden to argue with him, no matter what the circumstances, a situation that taught her to keep her words and emotions in check.

The Jordan girls felt cherished and secure, but they lived under extremely tight discipline. Religion came first, and in the Jordan home that meant all-day services on Sunday, no dancing, no comic books or novels. The Jordans strongly encouraged their children to read, but only such approved material as the Bible or schoolbooks. "Our parents helped us with homework," Rose Mary has said, "especially Dad. He played a major role there."

Benjamin Jordan measured Rose Mary by his toughest standards. He expected her to be home from her dates exactly on time, to excel in school, and, because he had, to go to college. Tall, thin, and striking, she resembled her father in manner and looks. Bennie and Barbara, pretty girls who were sometimes mistaken for twins, were tall, too, but more rounded in build.

All the daughters were close to their mother, who was not quite as strict as her husband. Once, secretly defying household rules, she allowed an older cousin to take the girls to a Shirley Temple movie. That was a red-letter day, the subject of hours of whispered conversations and smothered giggles. Even as adults, Barbara and her sisters kept a special place in their hearts for the dimpled, curly-haired star who sang "On the Good Ship Lollypop."

Benjamin Jordan would no doubt have frowned on that song, but he loved music and made it an important element in his family's life. He and his wife, both accomplished musicians, played the piano and sang well—mostly, of course, Baptist hymns. Insisting that all three girls take piano lessons, the Jordans

On the lookout for salable rags and scrap metal, junk dealer Patten guides his mules through a Houston back street. Barbara spent every Sunday helping her grandfather, who scrupulously shared his profits with her. "We got along famously," she said.

engaged a dedicated but tough teacher, Miss Mattie Thomas.

Thomas took no nonsense, demanding that her students practice every day and that they give yearly public recitals. Barbara was fond of music and enjoyed playing the guitar, but she hated the piano lessons and the performances. She submitted to Thomas's regimen for two years, then revolted. No more grueling hours of practice, she told Thomas, and no more miserable recitals. The astonished teacher rushed to Barbara's father; his daughter, she snorted, had treated her in a most "highhanded way."

Ben Jordan reacted to Thomas's complaint with predictable outrage. Not only had his youngest

The Jordan sisters (left to right), Bennie, Barbara, and Rose Mary, line up for a family-album shot in the early 1940s. Benjamin Jordan proudly told friends that his girls did not dance, play cards, read comic books, or go to the movies, a boast that Barbara resented. "How can he," she fumed, "go around bragging about the fact that he has three freaks?"

daughter shown disrespect to her elders; she had dared to disobey him! A family storm broke, but in the end, Barbara stood her ground. She and her father, both of them strong-willed and stubborn, would have many such clashes during her childhood years and beyond.

The two of them, in fact, "did not see eye to eye on anything," said Barbara Jordan. She recalled an occasion when she heard him talking to a friend about his daughters: "They don't drink, they don't smoke, they don't dance, they don't play cards, they don't go to the movies," said Preacher Jordan. His words, said his rebellious youngest child, "caused me the squeemies of the gut. I thought: 'How can he go around bragging about the fact that he has three freaks?'"

Next to his children's morality, nothing concerned Benjamin Jordan more than their education. "No man can take away your brain," he often told the girls. He wanted them to study, to think clearly, and to speak well. In love with language, he insisted that they pronounce English with precision and speak it with power and conviction. Here, Barbara did not disappoint him.

As she grew up, she actually overtook her father in zeal. If she got one B out of a row of A's on her report card, he was puzzled, but she was outraged. Nothing less than a straight-A average would satisify her.

"Barbara always had a mind of her own," recalled Rose Mary. "She was the driving force in the family." Armed with the values, discipline, and respect for hard work she learned from her father, Barbara developed her own strict code of principles. Her attitudes were further honed by the era of pervasive racial discrimination in which she grew up.

Most young Americans of today, black and white, know racism and segregation ruled the land before the civil rights movement of the mid-1950s and the 1960s. They may, however, find it hard to understand the degree to which racial discrimination affected the life of all Americans. Throughout Barbara Jordan's formative years, her skin color made her, in effect, a second-class citizen.

Discrimination found its way into every part of American life, in schools and restaurants and buses, in playgrounds and movie theaters, at beaches and ball games, in neighborhoods and apartment houses. If you were black, particularly in the South, you lived in segregated housing and sent your children to segregated schools. You rode in the back of the bus, and if a white person was standing, you gave up your seat. You used "colored" water fountains and rest rooms.

If you found yourself in a strange neighborhood or unfamiliar town, you might have trouble finding a place that would serve you food or rent you a room. You would, of course, try not to find yourself in an unfamiliar neighborhood. In places where white people made the rules, potential trouble always lurked. It might take the form of hostile stares or taunts from passing whites; it might be worse if a band of white supremacists—the Ku Klux Klan, for example—happened to be roaming around looking for "uppity blacks." A confrontation with these hooded terrorists could result in a beating or even in murder.

In Houston, as in other cities across the land, blacks freely entered "white territory" to work, perhaps as chauffeurs or nursemaids, but at the end of the day they left quickly. Their own segregated neighborhoods might be poor and shabby, but they were relatively free of suspicious white policemen eager to pick them up on any pretext at all.

Under these circumstances, most black parents understandably tried to keep their children close to home for as long as possible. As a result, the

youngsters often grew up with only a vague concept of the larger world. Barbara Jordan said that in her childhood, everyone she knew was poor and black, as she was herself. "Since I didn't see movies, and we didn't have television, and I didn't go anyplace with anybody else," she wrote in her autobiography, "how could I know anything else to consider?" For Barbara, the community of white people might as well have been on another planet.

The Jordan girls remained in their own segregated world far past childhood. When Rose Mary graduated from high school in 1949, she headed for Prairie View College, a nearby all-black institution. That same year, Barbara joined her other sister, Bennie, at Houston's all-black Phillis Wheatley High School. (The school was named for an African-born woman

Foreshadowing the civil rights movement of the 1960s, young people in Washington, D.C., demonstrate against lynching in the 1930s. Rampant social injustice occasionally sparked such protests, but the era's average American regarded racial discrimination as a fact of life.

who had arrived in Boston as a slave in 1753. Freed by her master when she was in her twenties, Wheatley had gone on to become the first published black American poet.)

Far brighter than average, Barbara enjoyed school. She established a strong-knit "gang," wore fashionable toeless shoes, had a smooth pageboy haircut, and rooted wildly for the school football team. ("I wasn't a cheerleader," she recalled, "but I should have been.") She disliked physical education—"I didn't want to put on the gym shorts," she said—but she did well in all her other classes and in her many extracurricular activities, especially debating.

Barbara's effectiveness as a debater came from more than the strong, resonant voice she inherited from her mother. Schooled by her father and grand-father, she demonstrated an unusually keen ability to marshal and articulate her arguments, enabling her to overwhelm debating opponents with a one-two punch: drama backed by logic.

Barbara entered—and frequently won—scores of formal debates, some of them with Wheatley students, some with teams from other local schools. Her high ratings propelled her to the 1952 Ushers Oratorical Contest, a Baptist-sponsored event held in Waco, Texas. Competing with star black speechmakers from high schools all over the state, Barbara won first prize: $50 and an expense-paid trip to the national contest in Chicago.

Escorted by her mother, the young woman from Campbell Street took a train to the Illinois city. Here, at the Greater Bethesda Baptist Church, she would do her best to outshine dozens of other contestants, all of them male. Wearing a long pink evening dress, Barbara took the stage to deliver an impassioned oration about "The Necessity for a Higher Education."

"Today's youth are living in a confused world," asserted the teenager. Then, addressing an imaginary opponent who would deny college admittance to qualified candidates, she rolled into high gear. "You are not only refusing to one out of two of the youth in this country the opportunity to do the work for which they have been preparing themselves," she said with conviction, "but you are also deliberately refusing to give them the intellectual and moral guidance they need and that the world of tomorrow is to need." Commenting on her speech afterward, Barbara said, "the main thing I was saying was: 'Folks, a higher education is on the way in. It's the only way out of the fix you're in.' "

Barbara was rather pleased with her oration, and she had a right to be. The *Houston Informer* for July 17, 1952, carried this story: "Miss Barbara Charline Jordan, daughter of the Reverend and Mrs. Benjamin M. Jordan of 4910 Campbell Street, added to her long list of oratorical awards [at] the National United Ushers Association of America. . . . Miss Jordan represented the state of Texas and . . . won first place, [receiving] a $200 scholarship to the school of her choice and a literary medal."

The *Informer*, which went on to note that "the talented young woman won praise and congratulations from educational circles all over the state," added that Barbara "had the distinction of having been chosen 'Girl of the Year' [at Wheatley], and is winner of the Julius Levy Oratorical Contest award. . . . She also holds three district and two state championship medals in Junior and Senior declamation, respectively, and a medal for outstanding accomplishments in speech."

Concluding its story, the newspaper quoted Barbara Jordan's comment on winning the national contest. "It's just another milestone I have passed," she said. "It's just the beginning." ❧

Houston's main shopping district (pictured in the early 1930s) was like foreign territory to young Jordan and her friends. "We would go downtown and there were people sitting and eating and enjoying themselves—and it was all a totally white world," she recalled. "My feeling was, well, this is just it. I guess it's always going to be this way."

3

TRAINING A "GOD-GIVEN TALENT"

Encouraged—Even Pushed—by their parents, all the Jordan girls would attend college. Rose Mary and Bennie decided that after graduation they would become music teachers, a reachable goal for young black women in Texas during the early 1950s. Such a career held no attraction for Barbara.

Most of Barbara's high school girlfriends planned to teach school, but that also failed to interest her. "I always wanted to be something unusual," she recalled. "I never wanted to be run-of-the-mill. For a while I thought about becoming a pharmacist, but then I thought, whoever heard of an outstanding pharmacist?"

A speaker at a Wheatley High School Career Day ended Barbara's indecision. Held each year in the school auditorium, Career Day brought students into contact with blacks who had succeeded in various professions. Visiting Wheatley in 1950 was Edith Sampson, a future judge who had been practicing law in Chicago since 1926 and who had been the first

Champions Barbara Jordan and her friend Otis King accept the 1955 TSU Intra-Mural Debate Trophy from Texas Southern University president Samuel Milton Nabrit. Jordan and King proved almost unbeatable as a team, but most contemporaries gave Jordan the edge. "She had," said one, "a God-given talent for speaking."

33

United Nations delegate Edith Spurlock Sampson arrives in New York City in 1950, the year she addressed students at Phillis Wheatley High School—and changed Jordan's life. Dazzled by the self-confident, 49-year-old Chicago attorney, the 14-year-old Houston sophomore decided that she, too, would study law—although at the time, she later admitted, "I had no fixed notion of what that was."

woman—of any race—to earn a law degree from Chicago's prestigious Loyola University. At the time she spoke to the Wheatley students, Sampson was an assistant state's attorney for Illinois and an alternate U.S. delegate to the United Nations.

Vastly impressed by the tall, self-possessed Chicago attorney, Barbara Jordan decided that she, too, would become a lawyer. "Or," she recalled with amusement, "something called a lawyer. I had no fixed notion of what that was." Ben Jordan, who had often told his daughters that they should pursue any career they thought they could handle, approved of Barbara's ambition.

Arlyne Jordan, however, was less enthusiastic. As any mother might, she worried about her child taking on a bruising battle—attempting to storm what was, in the early 1950s, a largely white, all-male bastion. On the other hand, Arlyne also knew her daughter; what Barbara made up her mind to accomplish, she would more than likely do.

In the end, both parents' faith in their daughter's abilities and determination placed them firmly behind her: Somehow she would become a lawyer. The immediate problem, of course, was money. The Jordans had managed to send Rose Mary and Bennie through college, and they would manage with Barbara. But now there would be three years of law school after college, a formidable challenge.

For economy's sake, Barbara and her parents decided she should attend a local college; living at home would save on transportation, room, and board. Accordingly, she applied to Texas Southern University (TSU), a small, relatively new, all-black Houston institution, and was accepted for the fall term of 1952.

Determined to make a big splash in her first year, Jordan ran for president of the TSU freshman class. She campaigned hard, delivering a number of campus speeches in her ringing voice, but when the votes were counted, the winner was Andrew Jefferson. Jordan and Jefferson would later become good friends, but she never conceded defeat. Many years later, Jefferson, by then a successful Houston attorney, smiled as he said, "She claims I stole that election from her to this day."

Jordan spent most of the time when she was not in class or at the library in extracurricular activities, mainly as a star member of the college debating team. But, like most of the era's college students, she also wanted to join a sorority. A strict Baptist, Ben Jordan flatly refused to finance such a "hellfire" activity, so Barbara financed her membership dues with a series of housecleaning and baby-sitting jobs. She began to spend occasional afternoons with her Delta Sigma

Patricia and Allan Bradford—along with their parents and millions of other Americans—await the outcome of Brown v. Board of Education, *the historic case argued before the Supreme Court (background) in May 1954. Until the* Brown *decision officially ended U.S. school segregation, most blacks, including Barbara Jordan, attended "separate but equal" schools.*

Theta sisters, roaring around town in their cars and gathering at such fashionable spas as the Groovy Grill.

TSU law professor Otis King, Barbara Jordan's college classmate and longtime friend, recalls the young Barbara as "a fun pal and a good dancer." She was, he said, "one of the best in our group. She was very light on her feet and she really enjoyed herself in a social situation."

Inevitably, Barbara's updated life-style led to trouble with her father. Spotting her "in a public place," seated at a table "littered" with bottle caps, one of Ben Jordan's parishioners raced off to tell the pastor. Barbara came home that evening to find her father in a rage. "What's the problem?" she asked. "I'll tell you what the problem is," he barked. "I have been informed that all you do at Texas Southern University is sit around and drink beer!"

Barbara now displayed an early flash of the political skill she later mastered. "Well, if somebody told you that's *all* we do," she responded coolly, "they lied." With that, she retired to her room, leaving her father, for once, speechless.

In truth, Barbara was far more conscientious than most of her classmates. Goal-minded and intense, she did not share her more popular peers' absorption in clothes, dates, and gossip, preferring to concentrate on sharpening the skills she knew she had. "Barbara dared to be different, even then," recalled her sister Rose Mary. "She aspired to roles that were not considered run-of-the-mill at that time." Otis King agreed: Basically, he said, college student Jordan was "a very serious person."

Jordan's greatest interest at college was the TSU debating team, and by her late teenage years she had developed truly impressive oratorical skills. Her voice was commanding and deep, her vocabulary extensive, her wit quick and sometimes biting. "She had a

God-given talent for speaking," recalled one colleague. Another contemporary, her onetime political opponent Andrew Jefferson, called her the "champion debater at TSU."

Under the leadership of TSU debate coach Tom Freeman, Jordan and her teammates toured the college debate circuit, taking on teams as far off as Chicago, Boston, and New York City. But Jordan had gotten her place on the team only after a struggle. It was not her skill that made Freeman hesitate about including her; it was her sex. He had always excluded women from his traveling group because, at the time, an unchaperoned female student touring with an all-male group would have raised eyebrows.

Such conventions were no match for Jordan's determination. Unwilling to miss anything, she set about downplaying her femininity and blending in with the rest of the team. All through her high school and early college days, she had worn frilly, scoop-necked dresses, piles of costume jewelry, open-toed

Texas Southern University (TSU) students relax on their tree-shaded campus in the mid-1950s. Responding to legal pressure for black equality in higher education, the Texas state legislature created TSU in 1947, five years before Jordan entered as a prelaw student.

Attempting to take seats at a lunch counter in Memphis, Tennessee, black students encounter a guardian of the establishment's all-white policy. During the mid-1950s, when Jordan toured with her college debating team, few restaurants served blacks. "You had to plan for food," recalled fellow debater Otis King, "and even plan ahead to locate service stations where blacks could use rest rooms."

shoes, and wavy, shoulder-length hair. Now she cut her hair short, gained weight, and affected loose, square-shouldered jackets and flat-heeled oxford shoes. As Shelby Hearon, cowriter of Jordan's autobiography, put it, "She became a no-nonsense presence, someone it was all right to take across the country in a carful of males and not worry about chaperonage."

During the years when it boasted Barbara Jordan, TSU won almost every debate it entered. In 1954, her junior year, this small, obscure southern college even tied mighty Harvard University, home of one of the nation's hottest debating teams. That year, Jordan received the Most Valuable Participant award at the Southern Intercollegiate Forensic Conference at Baylor University in Waco.

Travels with Freeman and the debating team were exciting events for Jordan. Discussing those days with an interviewer in 1991, Jordan's fellow debater Otis King recalled:

> The members of Professor Freeman's group hung out together. We called ourselves the Sigma Pi Alpha Forensic and Dialectical Symposium, and from that group, four or five members were chosen as the debating team for a particular event. Barbara and I were debating partners; we traveled around the country [in Freeman's yellow Mercury] and debated such themes as the guaranteed annual wage. The debating trips were a lot of fun. We played word games as we traveled, spelling games, counting games.

In the more serious debates, said King, "Barbara was always a tremendous speaker, always had that big voice. I recall once in Iowa that one of the judges said that she was too aggressive and her voice was too strong!" Sternly ruling that Jordan had not been "sufficiently ladylike," the judge gave the highest mark for the debate to another contender.

To warm up before their major contests, Freeman's team often gave exhibition debates, sometimes in high schools. King remembered a few of the more lighthearted contests, such as Resolved: A Woman's Place Is in the Home. "Barbara was very good at things like that," King said. "She was very good at coming up with quips. She had a fine light side and we just had a lot of fun."

These carefree days, however, were sometimes darkened by the ugliness of racial discrimination. King recalled that side of the debating tours as well:

> There was strict segregation in the South at that time, so we had to travel from place to place based on where we could stay. We spent long stretches in the car because there was nowhere to stay in between. We would buy food at grocery stores and eat in the car unless we found a black-run restaurant or a restaurant that would serve blacks around through the back. Occasionally, we would find a place where blacks were allowed to come in the back door and sit and eat in the kitchen. You had to plan for food and even plan ahead to locate service stations where blacks could use rest rooms.

These conditions began to change while Jordan was still in college, but change came slowly. In 1954, attorney Thurgood Marshall of the National Association for the Advancement of Colored People (NAACP) went to the Supreme Court with a case called *Brown v. Board of Education of Topeka*. Marshall, a veteran battler for civil rights, convinced the Supreme Court that segregated public schools could never provide black children with the equal education that the law guaranteed all citizens. Ordered to integrate their schools, southern states moved with extreme reluctance, but eventually they did move.

As she read about attorney Marshall's dazzling Supreme Court performance, Jordan began to think seriously about where to apply for her own law training. The debate with Harvard convinced her to apply to Harvard Law School, probably the nation's most prestigious legal educational institution. "I want to go to the best," she told Coach Freeman, "and Harvard is the best."

Gently but firmly, Freeman explained the facts of academic life, 1950s style. "You can't get in Harvard," he told her. "They have never heard of Texas Southern University at Harvard Law School." However, said Freeman, in light of Jordan's excellent grades, she might be accepted at Boston University (BU) Law School, also a top-notch training ground. "Well," said Jordan dubiously, "I'll write to Boston."

When she received the Boston University Law School catalogs, Jordan made a list all the expenses—books, tuition, room and board—she would face, then brought the material to her father. "This is where I want to go to law school," she said.

Ben Jordan had yearned for a college degree for himself. A gifted student from Edna, Texas, he had applied to Booker T. Washington's legendary Tuskegee Institute at the urging of his mother, a Baptist missionary. To his delight, Tuskegee took him, and he spent three years studying, playing football, and making his mother glow with pride. Then she became

Beaming with pride, TSU debate coach Tom Freeman and his star performer examine the varsity debating team's latest trophies. Freeman, an inspiring but realistic professor, advised Jordan to forget her dream of exclusive Harvard Law School and try for more attainable Boston University, which accepted her as a law student in 1956.

mortally ill; Ben had to leave school before his graduation. He came home and, after his mother's death, moved to Houston and took a job as a warehouse clerk.

Now his daughter—sometimes called "the black sheep of the family"—stood before him with shining eyes and a mind-boggling budget. He read the papers she had given him, looked up at her, then, as she put it later, "offered all he had." Speaking gruffly, Ben Jordan said, "This is more money than I have ever spent on anything or anyone. But if you want to go, we'll manage."

Boston University accepted Jordan, who graduated from TSU magna cum laude in 1956. Two months later, filled with excitement, fear, and high hopes, she headed north. She had done some traveling, but only with her mother or her college associates, and she had always lived at home. This move was, she said, "my first departure from the womb." ❧

4

"THE WAY TO SUCCEED"

TALL, SERIOUS, DETERMINED—and frightened half to death—Barbara Jordan arrived in Boston in the fall of 1956. She was about to begin the three toughest years she had yet experienced. First of all, she knew she would not see a familiar face for many months. "If I pay for you to go up there," her father had told her, "there won't be any money for you to come home for Thanksgiving, Christmas, Easter. Once you get there, you're there." Now she was *there*.

Founded in 1869 and situated across the Charles River from Harvard, Boston University was a first-rate law school that could give Jordan an excellent legal education. BU was also expensive and offered no scholarships for which Jordan qualified. She was keenly aware that her enrollment had prompted real sacrifices from her whole family, all of whom pitched in to help their beloved "black sheep." Rose Mary, for example, had just started working when her sister entered law school. "I would get a little paycheck," she recalled, "and send a little something to help out with extras Barbara might need."

Black and female, 20-year-old Jordan felt like a fish out of water when she entered predominantly white, almost entirely male Boston University Law School in 1956. On her first shaky night in Boston, she looked into her dormitory mirror and asked an anguished question: "What in the world, Barbara Jordan, are you doing here?"

Boston University (pictured in the 1950s), which attracted students from first-class eastern schools, made Jordan view her own education as woefully inadequate. "Separate was not equal," she said of segregated schooling, then set about doing what she called "16 years of remedial work in thinking."

From their modest schoolteachers' salaries, Rose Mary and Bennie each sent their sister $10 per month. "I figured I could make it on that," Barbara Jordan noted. "Forty cents a day for the subway, and the food was paid for, and I would have a little left over for a movie."

Jordan vowed to repay her parents and sisters by proving herself worthy of their confidence in her. At the moment, however, her own confidence seemed a bit shaky. She never forgot settling into her room on the night of her arrival and asking the mirror a question: "What in the world, Barbara Jordan, are you doing here?"

Jordan experienced something of a culture shock when she met the other freshman law students: There were 5 women—1 of whom was black—and 592 white men. Furthermore, all these strangers seemed to know things Jordan did not. Most had attended solidly established eastern schools and colleges, and most had spent their summers working for lawyers, usually their fathers. To Jordan, all the words she was now hearing—*promisor, promisee, tort, lessor, lessee*—sounded like a foreign tongue. To her fellow students, she said, this language "was so familiar, it was just like mother's milk."

With awful clarity, Jordan began to see that neither all her years of schooling nor all her top grades had prepared her to compete with or even to keep up with her mostly white colleagues. "The best training available in an all-black instant university," she wrote, "was not equal to the best training one developed as a white university student." As Thurgood Marshall had so eloquently pointed out, segregated schools could never provide quality education. "No matter what kind of face you put on it or how many frills you attached to it," said Jordan, "separate was not equal. I was doing 16 years of remedial work in thinking."

In the past, she noted in her autobiography, "I had got along by spouting off. I really had not had my ideas challenged ever." At BU, she now saw, "you had to think and read and understand and reason." This, she added, "was a new thing for me. I cannot, I really cannot describe what that did to my insides and to my head. I thought: I'm being educated finally."

Jordan had studied hard for her first midyear examination, and she approached it with some confidence. Once she saw it, however, she knew she was in trouble. She sweated through pages of complex, deliberately ambiguous questions, answered them as best she could, then walked out in despair, certain that she had "punched out." Stumbling half-blindly into a nearby movie theater, she sat in the dark for three hours, wondering "how I was going to lay it on my father that I had just busted out of law school."

The test score turned out to be a 79, the lowest grade Jordan had ever received but well above failing. From that point on, the young Texan began to study harder than anyone else in the school. "It was not a matter of trying to catch up," she said. "You couldn't.

Howard Thurman was a prolific author and noted theologian, as well as a persuasive mystic and spellbinding orator. Jordan, who listened to him preach all through her years at Boston University Law School, said his sermons "were focused on the present time that all of us were having difficulty coming to grips with."

What you wanted to do was slot right in where you were and deal with that, and you knew that you had to work extraordinarily hard to function right there, where you were."

Embarrassed by her educational needs, Jordan did most of her reading in an upstairs room of a graduate dormitory instead of in the law library. Every night after dinner, she loaded her books under her arm and trudged off to her sanctuary, often staying up until daylight. "I didn't get much sleep during those years," she said later. "I was lucky if I got three or four hours a night, because I had to stay up. I had to."

The first year was the hardest, but the remaining two saw little letup in Jordan's labors. "I worked my tail to the bone," she said. In time, she managed to find occasional hours when she could meet friends and play the guitar. She also found time for church on Sundays. Religion had not been "liberating" to her, she said, until she "got out from under the careful watch of the Reverend Benjamin M. Jordan." Now she found herself going to chapel services because she wanted to, not because she had to.

Listening to weekly sermons preached by noted black clergyman Howard Thurman, Jordan decided that "God really is caring. He wants me to live according to the preachments of His scripture, but He doesn't mean for me to be hounded into heaven. He just wants me to live right and treat other people right." Thurman so affected Jordan that for a while she considered switching to divinity school. Eventually, however, she settled for faith plus a law degree.

When she realized that she had indeed qualified for that degree, Jordan called her family but told them not to think of spending the money to attend her graduation services. Thrilled by her news, the Jordans paid no attention to her advice. In June 1959, Arlyne, Ben, Rose Mary (now Mrs. John McGowan), and Bennie jumped into the family car for the long drive to Boston.

On graduation day, Barbara Jordan opened a scroll tied with a red ribbon: She had earned an LLB (*legum baccalaureus*, or bachelor of laws) degree from Boston University Law School. Along with the rest of her proud family, she cried. Well, you've done it, thought Jordan. You've really done it. Then, she said, "We all went out and had a celebration."

After graduation, Jordan decided to take the Massachusetts bar examination (the test that any prospective lawyer must pass before being licensed to work in a given state) and then settle in Boston. In three years, she had grown used to life in a racially integrated community: "The air is freer up here," she said.

But after a summer in her adopted city—she earned her living by working as a BU dormitory housemother—Jordan found she missed Texas, segregation notwithstanding. She wanted to go home. Her mother greeted the telephoned news with joy. "Thank God," she said, explaining that she had been on her knees, praying hard for her daughter's return. "Well," said Jordan with a smile, "I didn't know I had all *that* working against me when I was doing my best to stay."

Back home in Houston, Jordan took the Texas bar exam; passed it; ordered a batch of cards that read BARBARA JORDAN, Attorney at Law; and opened her first office—a space on the family dining table on Campbell Street. She got some business, but she still found herself with free time, so she volunteered her services to the Harris County Democratic Committee. After working to bring out the vote in the 1960 election, in which Bostonian John F. Kennedy and Texan Lyndon B. Johnson defeated former vice-president Richard M. Nixon and diplomat Henry Cabot Lodge, Jordan made a self-discovery: "I had really been bitten by the political bug."

The campaign had also taught the 24-year-old lawyer that her debater's skills translated beautifully to the political stump. When she took the stage, people listened. A year after the campaign, she moved into her own office, a downtown Houston room shared with another young attorney. By this time, she had gained some fame in Harris County. The only woman in the all-black Houston Lawyers Association, she had been elected to its presidency. She had also been named second vice-chairman of the Harris County Democrats and was a member of the Houston Council on Human Relations.

Equipped with balloons, posters, and beribboned hats, delegates crowd the floor at the 1960 Democratic National Convention. That year's slate—Senator John F. Kennedy of Massachusetts and Senator Lyndon B. Johnson of Texas—captured the interest of young attorney Jordan, who volunteered to make speeches for the local Democratic organization.

Encouraged by friends, 68-year-old Tom Flowers registers to cast the first ballot of his life. Rounding up new voters became one of Jordan's specialties: The fledgling politician and her colleagues managed to get 80 percent of Harris County's black voters to the polls in 1960. By then, she said, "I had really been bitten by the political bug."

In 1962, Jordan decided to run for a seat in the Texas House of Representatives. After borrowing the $500 filing fee required of candidates, she asked herself a pointed question: Do you really understand the way Texas state government functions? The answer was no. The fledgling politician found a thick textbook on the subject and read it from cover to cover, absorbing mountains of data on what she called "the rules of the game in the state of Texas." Then, formulating a basic campaign speech based on "retrenchment and reform" of state government, she hit the campaign trail.

Crisscrossing Harris County, she spoke to anyone who would listen about the evils of discrimination and the needs and aspirations of the American people, especially those who were black. Audiences responded to Jordan's fiery speeches with applause and standing ovations, but in the end not enough of them cast their ballots for her.

Jordan garnered an impressive 46,000 votes, but her opponent, a white lawyer named Willis Whatley, got 65,000. Although she won some white votes, most of Jordan's supporters had been black. "The votes were just not there from these fine white people," she noted. "That was very puzzling to me."

A political expert gave Jordan a depressing analysis: "You've got too much going against you," he said. "You're black, you're a woman, and you're large. People don't really like that image." This made little sense to Jordan, but, she said, she "tucked that away, as something to remember."

In 1964, Jordan ran again—and lost again. She asked herself another question: Is politics worth staying in for me? This time the answer was a resounding yes. She wanted to gain a voice in government, a position from which she could help engineer the changes she felt her race, her state, and her country needed. "I did not like losing," she said.

Campaigning for Texas state representative in 1962, Jordan makes the first of two unsuccessful bids for elective office. After her defeat, a political expert suggested she had three strikes against her—"You're black, you're a woman, and you're large"—but she refused to give up. "I did not like losing," she said. "I intended to devote my full attention to figuring out the way to succeed."

"I intended to devote my full attention to figuring out the way to succeed."

One way to ensure success, counseled friends, family, and political advisers, was to get married. Jordan came to see that, whereas the public never expected a male candidate to "care for the babies, or iron the curtains, or clean the johns," it did expect a woman to have, "over and above and beyond other aspirations, a home and a family."

Jordan weighed the alternatives. Politics had come to mean more to her than anything else, and, she said, "I did not want anything to take away from the singleness of my focus." She would press on, seeking a political career and doing her best to "bring the public along to understand that there are some women for whom other expectations [than marriage] are possible."

Would the white-dominated voting districts of conservative, traditional, segregated Houston ever elect a statuesque, black, unmarried woman? An easy question, said people who understood southern politics: The answer was no.

Barbara Jordan had other ideas. As it turned out, so did the U.S. Supreme Court. ⌖

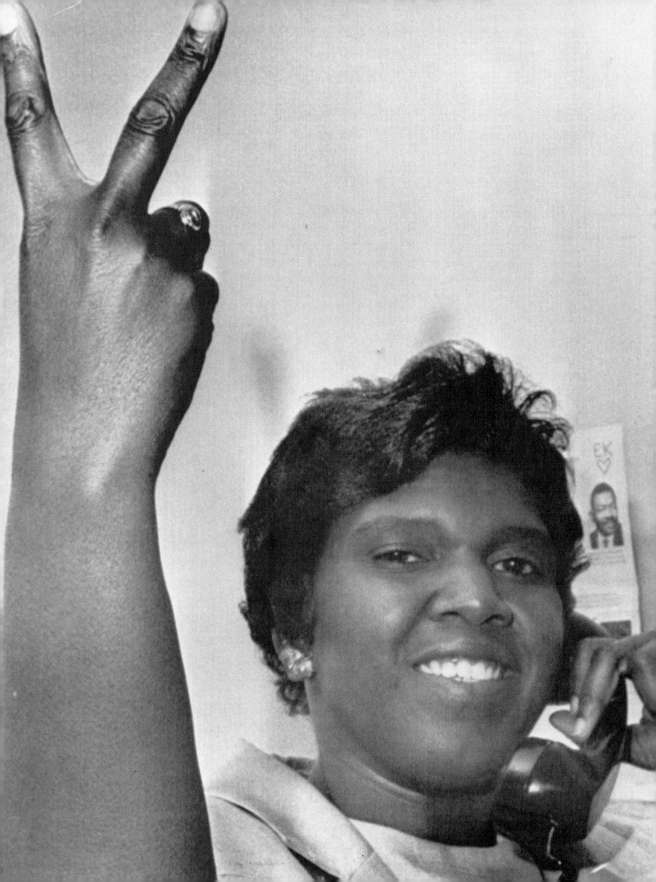

5

A LONE STAR
IN THE
SENATE

◀●▶

Barbara Jordan decided in 1965 to launch a third campaign for political office. This time, however, she did not seek to become a state representative. She set her sights on the position of state senator.

Over the past three years, the U.S. Supreme Court had ruled on a half-dozen cases that changed the way a number of voting districts, including those in Harris County, were set up. It was not constitutional, the Supreme Court stated, for legislative districts to be established according to county lines; rather, a region's population should determine the borders of each voting district. In effect, these court decisions affirmed the constitutional principle of equal representation for equal numbers of people. One person's vote should count just as much as another's, regardless of his or her race.

When the state of Texas was forced to reshape its legislative districts in 1965, Jordan found herself in the newly formed 11th State Senatorial District. Thirty-eight percent of the people who lived in the district were black; the rest of the population consisted of Chicanos and working-class whites. As it turned out, the new district also contained most of the precincts that had voted for Jordan in the two previous campaigns. These factors encouraged her to run for a seat in the state senate, even though no black had served as a Texas state senator in the 20th century. Nor had a black woman ever campaigned for the post.

To file as a candidate cost $1,000. This time, Jordan did not have to borrow any money to pay the filing fee. Since 1964, she had been working at two

Blacks line up to vote at an Alabama country store in 1966, soon after a U.S. Supreme Court decision forced several southern states to redesign their electoral districts. The reorganization produced more black voters, who, in turn, elected more black officials—one of whom was Barbara Jordan of Harris County, Texas.

jobs: her Lyons Avenue law practice, which was small but growing; and her full-time position as administrative assistant to Bill Elliot, the county judge. Jordan resigned from the post she held with Elliot in December 1965, accepted a salaried job as director of a nonprofit foundation to help "hard-core unemployables," and then used money she had saved from all three positions to file as a candidate for the state senate on February 4, 1966.

Opposing Jordan as a candidate in the Democratic primary was Charles Whitfield, who had already served for eight years in the senate. To some observers, it appeared that Jordan was beaten even before she began her campaign. Whitfield was a white male who had been backed by the Harris County Democratic Committee every time he ran for office. And he supported many of the causes that Jordan did. How could she expect to unseat him?

Realizing that she had to campaign even harder than she had in her previous attempts to get elected, Jordan set up her headquarters in the True Level Lodge Building on Lyons Avenue—right near her law office—and went to work. Making good use of her speechmaking ability and pointing out that she was a black candidate in a heavily black legislative district, she persuaded the Harris County Democratic Committee to endorse her instead of Whitfield. For the first time in the 30-year-old Jordan's political career, being black was a help, not a hindrance. "Black votes made the difference for her," acknowledged a committee member.

Whitfield, however, was not a gracious loser. At a Democratic Committee meeting in March, he denounced Jordan as being unqualified to represent the people in the 11th District. Jordan also attended the meeting, and upon hearing her rival's words she rose from her seat and said in a sure and powerful voice, "I live in this district and I was born in this district and these are the people I am representative of." Her brief speech earned her a standing ovation and confirmed to the committee that it had put itself behind the right candidate.

"I would not allow myself to believe it," Jordan said of her chances of winning the election, "for fear I would not work as hard." Convinced that she had to keep the pressure on Whitfield, she sent out sample ballots to all 35,000 black voters in the 11th District. She included instructions explaining how to fill out the ballots with a vote cast for Barbara Jordan.

Whitfield launched a counterattack. Complaining about what he called the "black block vote," he introduced the topic of race into the election. "Can a white man win?" he asked repeatedly, until it became his campaign slogan. "Shall we have a seat for a member of the NEGRO race," he asked in his campaign flyers, "or shall we consider other factors such as qualifications and experience in order to give Harris County its most effective voice in the 11th District?"

As it turned out, Whitfield would probably have been better off talking about his record as a legislator. His attempts to cut down Jordan proved to be a mistake. Responding to her rival's claim of a black block vote, she told the people of the 11th District: "Don't tell us about black block votes. You know white folks have been block-voting for the past century. We don't have to apologize. Our time has come!" An experienced debater, Jordan began to conclude her campaign speech by turning the tables on Whitfield: "My opponent asks, 'Can a white man win?' And I say to you, 'NO, NOT THIS TIME. NOT . . . THIS . . . TIME!"

She was right. On May 8, 1966, Jordan sat with her mother and father and watched the Democratic primary returns roll in. Before long, the incoming election results indicated that she had gained an

President Lyndon B. Johnson campaigns for a fellow Texan. Describing Jordan as "the epitome of the new politics," Johnson said she had "proved that black is beautiful before we knew what it meant." She was, he continued, "involved in a governmental system of all the people, all the races, all economic groups."

insurmountable lead. Jordan then turned to her parents and said, "All right, let's get dressed and get down to the True Level Lodge for a celebration. I've just wiped him out." She had indeed. Jordan defeated Whitfield by a margin of nearly two votes to one.

Along with another election-day winner, 27-year-old Curtis M. Graves, Jordan was about to become the first black in 84 years to take a seat in the Texas legislature. (Under normal circumstances, both Jordan and Graves would face a Republican opponent in the general elections held on November 8. But no Republicans were going to run against the two Democrats, so Jordan and Graves were assured of their respective seats in the state senate and the Texas House of Representatives.) She took the oath of office on January 10, 1967, in Austin, the state

capital, and thus became the first black state senator in Texas since 1883.

Welcoming her into the Texas legislature on that historic day were hundreds of blacks who had traveled to Austin solely to congratulate Jordan and wish her well. Her family members were in attendance, too. They sat in the senate gallery and cheered Jordan when she entered the chamber. "I looked up at them and covered my lips with my index finger," she recalled. "They became quiet instantly, but continued to communicate their support by simply smiling. Finally I had won the right to represent a portion of the people in Texas."

Having successfully broken into the white, male-dominated world of Texas politics, Jordan now had to contend with the "good ol' boys" in the senate.

Jordan (front left), the Texas senate's only black member, prepares to respond to a roll call in 1966. Already conspicuous in her home state, the young lawmaker attracted national attention when President Johnson, passing over a number of more prominent civil rights leaders, invited her to the White House for a private preview of his proposed 1967 civil rights legislation.

"The Texas senate was touted as the state's most exclusive club," she said. "To be effective, I had to get inside the club, not just inside the chamber. I singled out the most influential and powerful members and was determined to gain their respect."

She won them over quickly. "I recall at one of our first receptions," she said in *Barbara Jordan: A Self-Portrait*, "a group of senators was talking, and as I walked up one was saying: 'And you know that no good son-of-a-bitch.' And by this time he had noticed that I was there, and he said, 'Barbara, I am so sorry, I am so sorry.' I said: 'If a person is a no good son-of-a-bitch, then he's a no good son-of-a-bitch.' So he said, 'Well, okay,' and went right on with his story. And I didn't try to use salty language because that would make me one of them, but I just wanted them to be comfortable, and not to keep saying: 'Excuse me,' 'Pardon me.'"

Jordan spent the better part of her first month on the job learning the complicated rules and procedures under which the 31-person Texas senate operated. Every day in the senate, she observed the finer points of these rules. At night, in the two-bedroom apartment she rented near the capitol, she studied legislative handbooks to help speed up the learning process.

Back in her law school days, Jordan had discovered "that you can't work all the time. You can't maintain a public face all the time. You need friends you can be with who don't care what your title is." Accordingly, she established a circle of people with whom she felt at ease.

The most notable relationship Jordan formed during this period, however, was with Texas's leading politician, President Lyndon Johnson. One month into her two-year term as state senator, the president invited her to Washington, D.C., to discuss a fair-housing bill. Several of the nation's leading civil rights leaders, among them Roy Wilkins and Whitney

Young, had also been invited to the White House meeting. But a number of other influential civil rights figures had not, including Stokely Carmichael, Floyd McKissick, and Bayard Rustin. That made Jordan's being invited all the more impressive.

At one point during this February 13 summit, Johnson turned to Jordan and asked for her opinion of the proposed fair-housing bill. "Well, Mr. President," she said, "this seems like a proper time to move on this legislation. It won't be easy. It will take work."

It was not the most passionate speech that Jordan, admittedly a bit overwhelmed by the moment, ever made. Still, she managed to make a good impression on the president, which was no easy accomplishment. "Lyndon Johnson was the prototype of the Texas

Backed by the Stars and Stripes and the Lone Star flag of Texas, Jordan exchanges greetings with fellow Texas politician Calvin Guest in the state capitol in Austin. To be an effective senator, Jordan realized she needed to be part of the "good ol' boys" network: To achieve that goal, she said, "I singled out the most influential and powerful members and was determined to gain their respect."

politician," she said later. "Tough, expansive, and pragmatic." He was also wise enough to recognize that Jordan was a rising star on the political scene, and over the next two years he consulted her periodically, inviting her to several White House functions (an honor not usually extended to a state senator) and appointing her to a spot on a special economic commission.

Jordan's star continued to rise in March 1967, when she made her first speech on the senate floor. "Rather than make a speech about oppression daily, I singled out one issue," she said. "I felt people in a very bottom way were fair, and I felt I could appeal to this fairness and reasonableness in my colleagues when the right matter came along."

The issue she singled out was taxes. A proposal had been made to add a one percent city sales tax on top of the state sales tax. Jordan felt the added tax would do more harm than good. "Texas is number one in poor people because of its regressive tax structure," she said on the senate floor. "The poor people of this state pay approximately thirty percent of their income in taxes. Where is the equity when the people who make the most pay the least, and the people who make the least pay the most?"

Even though Jordan's rousing speech failed to muster enough support to kill the proposal, it got her started in the state senate, and she was soon making her mark. When she presented her first bill, which fought discrimination in the workplace, it passed by a vote of 30 to 1.

After that, Jordan fought a voter registration bill requiring would-be voters to indicate if they could write their name and if a physical disability prevented them from marking the ballot. The proposed bill, she told her fellow state senators, "is alien to the concept that the right to vote ought to be easily accessible and available to all people with minimum details and procedures for registering." To defeat the bill, she got the backing of 10 other state senators, and their combined votes were enough to stop the legislation from being passed. Later in her first session in the state senate, she played a pivotal role in blocking a spending bill proposed by powerful Texas governor John Connally.

For her efforts, Jordan was named Outstanding Freshman Senator by her colleagues when the legislative session came to an end. On May 27, the other 30 state senators went so far as to pass a resolution honoring Jordan. The resolution was read aloud on the senate floor. Jordan, it said, "has earned the esteem and respect of her fellow senators by the dignified manner in which she has conducted herself while serving in the legislature, and because of her sincerity, her genuine concern for others, and her forceful ability, and she has been a credit to her state as well as to her race."

Deeply moved by the occasion, Jordan told her co-workers, "When I came here on the 10th day of January, you were all strangers. There were perhaps mutual suspicions, tensions, and apprehensions. Now, I believe they have been replaced by mutual respect."

She had clearly won the respect of the voters. In 1968, Jordan ran unopposed for a second term and was easily reelected. This time, because there was no longer the need to stagger the state senator's term in office because of redistricting, she would be serving for four years rather than two. ❧

6

"I WAS
THE GOVERNOR"

AS IN HER first term as a state senator, Barbara Jordan took on an extremely large work load. She was appointed to serve on 10 different government committees and took part in a variety of other important meetings, such as the Southern Conference of State Governments and the Interim Committee for Urban Affairs. She also traveled around the country to speak to various groups about the state of race relations in the United States.

By the late 1960s, the civil rights movement had become caught in what one of its leaders, A. Philip Randolph, called "a crisis of victory." The movement had successfully battled segregation in public facilities and other forms of racial discrimination through direct nonviolent action. But other problems, such as the concerns of the black poor, who were often caught in generational cycles of poverty, could not be remedied with nonviolent protests that merely opened up opportunities. A growing segment of black America advocated the use of force to attain actual

Jordan ponders an often-asked question: Why did she not take a more militant stand in the battle for racial equality? "All blacks are militant in their guts," the legislator—who had sponsored a record number of social-reform bills—once explained, "but militancy is expressed in different ways."

equal rights. Many blacks urged Jordan to join their fight and become more militant, but she refused. "We have failed to heal the gap between the middle-class black lawyer and the black slum dweller," she told the members of the black National Bar Association. "We must exchange the philosophy of excuses—what I am is beyond my control—for the philosophy of responsibility. We should tell the citizen that a man of liberty does not burn down the neighborhood store, then beg for his supper. We should tell him that a citizen of dignity does not wait for the world to give him anything."

The only way to solve racial problems was through reason and understanding, Jordan maintained. "Most Negroes have a little black militancy swimming around in them," she said, "and most white people have a little Ku Klux Klan swimming around in them. If we'd be honest with each other, we would discover we are all victims of racism that is historically a part of this country."

In the midst of such pleas, the civil rights movement lost two of its major players. On the evening of April 4, 1968, Martin Luther King, Jr., was felled by an assassin's bullet outside a motel room in Memphis, Tennessee; the silencing of the movement's leading voice left the nation without a clearcut choice for black leader. Around the same time, President Lyndon Johnson, a powerful supporter of civil rights, announced his decision not to run for another term in office.

That same year, Jordan traveled to Chicago to take part in her first Democratic National Convention. As a delegate from Texas, she was to help choose the party's presidential candidate. With Johnson out of the running, Hubert H. Humphrey was nominated for the presidency, only to lose in the national election that November to Republican candidate Richard Nixon.

Meanwhile, Jordan continued to keep busy at the Texas senate, attending committee meetings, orchestrating major pieces of legislation, including labor-management bills for both a workmen's compensation package and unemployment compensation, a bill to guarantee equal rights for women, a bill to form a department of labor in the state, and a bill to create a nonprofit corporation that would lend people money for low-income housing.

Midway through her second term, Jordan was cited by *Harper's Bazaar* as "a gifted, able orator" and was placed on the magazine's list of "One Hundred Women in Touch with Our Time." Her hometown of Houston honored her, too, proclaiming October 1, 1971, as Barbara Jordan Day.

Later that month, Jordan held a fund-raising event in downtown Houston to help finance an upcoming political campaign. A new congressional district had just been formed in Texas, after a recent shift in the state's population caused the state to be redistricted. This new district was made up largely of the people who had voted Jordan into the state senate, and in 1972 they would be electing a representative for Congress. Jordan planned on being that person.

Curtis Graves wanted to be elected the new congressman, too. Elected to the Texas House of Representatives at the same time that Jordan was voted into the state senate, Graves had made a bid to become mayor of Houston three years earlier. He had lost that campaign; he did not intend to lose again.

"Senator Jordan has demonstrated a blind loyalty to the Democratic Party machine," Graves said in August 1971, preparing the way to announce his candidacy for the 18th Congresional District seat. "[She] has seldom involved herself in anything controversial, let alone anything controversial concerning the black community." He was making it clear to Jordan that if she chose to challenge him for the new seat, she would find herself in the political fight of her life.

Jordan, however, was eager to meet his challenge. To get her campaign rolling, she donned a fetching gold-and-brown gown and hosted a fund-raiser at the grand ballroom of the Rice Hotel. The event attracted 1,500 people; the evening's guest list included a large number of family members, longtime friends, and influential Texans, including Lieutenant Governor Ben Barnes and Houston mayor Louie Welch, both of whom made speeches in praise of Jordan.

The highlight of the evening was an appearance by former president Johnson. "Barbara Jordan proved to us that black is beautiful before we knew what that meant," he told the crowd. "She is a woman of keen intellect and unusual legislative ability, a symbol proving that 'We Can Overcome.' . . . Those with hurting consciences because they have discriminated against blacks and women can vote for Barbara Jordan and feel good." (Johnson later sent her a private note that said, "I'm delighted that I was able to share the reception with you and pay tribute to one of the most capable, caring ladies I know.")

Spurred by the success of the fund-raiser, Jordan formally entered the race in December 1971. Over

Bennie Jordan Creswell (left) and Rose Mary Jordan McGowan (right) congratulate their little sister after her May 1972 victory in the Democratic primary, which assured her of a seat in the U.S. House of Representatives. "Back in December when I entered this race, I promised to represent all the people of the 18th District, black, white, brown, young and old, rich and poor," Jordan told ecstatic followers. "I have received support and votes from all those groups . . . and I'm deeply grateful for it."

the course of the next half year, Graves tried to attack her as someone who has "brought our state into national shame and ridicule." He claimed that Jordan had sold out to corrupt politicians. She deflected each criticism gracefully. Never stooping to Graves's level of dirty politics, she ran on the strength of her record as a state senator.

It was more than enough. On May 6, 1972, Jordan won the Democratic primary handily, netting 80 percent of the vote. Her Republican opponent in the November election would fall almost as easily.

In the meantime, Jordan finished out her term in the state senate. On June 10, the members of the Texas legislature accorded her a rare privilege. They made Jordan governor of Texas for a day.

Periodically, the Texas senate elects a president pro tem to serve as an assistant to the lieutenant governor. Whoever is chosen as president pro tem is supposed to assume the mantle of governor when the governor and his immediate successor, the lieutenant governor, are both out of the state. In Texas, it has become a tradition for the governor and lieutenant governor to leave the state deliberately for one day so the president pro tem can spend a day as governor.

Jordan was elected president pro tem in late March 1972. A week after the Democratic primary, Governor Preston Smith and Lieutenant Governor Barnes arranged to be out of the state so Jordan could have her day. She began her 24 hours as governor by breakfasting at the governor's mansion with everyone in her family except her father, who was suffering from a heart condition. He had driven to Austin with the other family members but had decided to skip the breakfast so he would be well rested for the events that were to follow.

Sure enough, Benjamin Jordan was ready at 9:30 in the morning, when his youngest daughter entered the capitol to be sworn in as governor. He stood

alongside Barbara as an old TSU friend, Judge Andrew Jefferson, administered the oath in full view of all the state senators. To Jordan's great satisfaction, the gallery was packed with her friends and well-wishers. "You could not even squeeze a gnat through the door," she remembered with pleasure. "And they could yell and they could applaud to their hearts' content. I did not have to tell them to be quiet, because I was governor, and I could run my day the way I wanted to."

Barbara Jordan, representative-to-be from Texas's 18th Congressional District, gets a hug from her two strongest supporters. For Arlyne and Benjamin Jordan, the 1972 primary victory amply justifed their unswerving faith in their daughter, once known as the family's "black sheep."

Judge Andrew L. Jefferson, Jordan's old friend and college political adversary, swears her in as Texas "governor for a day" in June 1972. At that moment, Jordan became—if only for 24 hours—the first black woman to serve as chief of any American state.

The rest of the swearing-in ceremony included a military escort, a performance by a choir, and speeches by Leon Jaworski, president of the American Bar Association, and an address by Jordan herself. "The future can mean a bold new venture for Texas," she told her listeners. "It can mean an end to poverty and human suffering. The future can signal the beginning of a new commitment by the government of the state of Texas to the people of the state of Texas. . . . My faith in this state and its people makes me optimistic that this commitment will be made and fulfilled."

Next, the ceremonies moved to her new office in the capitol, where Jordan signed several proclamations and greeted the hundreds of visitors who had come to offer their congratulations. In the midst of all this activity, her oldest sister, Rose Mary, came over to say, "Daddy got sick. There is nothing to worry about, but we've taken him to the hospital. Mother has gone with him." Jordan attended the barbecue luncheon held in her honor, then went to Brackenridge Hospital to check on her father's condition. There she learned that he had suffered a stroke.

Benjamin Jordan's condition worsened overnight, and he died the next morning. "You know," Barbara told a friend afterward, "if my father had had the option of choosing a time to die, he would have chosen that day." He had lived to see his daughter become the first black woman governor of a state, even if it had been just for one day. ❧

7

"I THINK YOU SHOULD RUN FOR PRESIDENT"

———— ✦ ————

WHEN THE 93RD Congress of the United States convened on January 3, 1973, the House of Representatives included a freshman from Texas: 36-year-old Barbara Charline Jordan, the first black congresswoman from any southern state. Probably only half-joking, Jordan had expressed regret that she was not the first black congresswoman, period. That honor had gone to Shirley Chisholm of New York City, elected to the House in 1968 at the age of 44.

With four other newcomers to the House, Jordan had just completed a month at what she called Harvard Head Start—a program at Harvard University's John F. Kennedy Institute of Politics aimed at teaching first-time U.S. representatives about the ways of Congress.

Members of the House, traditionally male, had always been identified as "the gentleman from . . ." At Harvard, Jordan learned that she would be referred to as "the gentlelady from Texas." Jordan did not much care for the word, but she decided there were more important things to worry about. Gentlelady it would be.

The House, with its 435 legislators, represented an overwhelming contrast to the 31-member Texas senate; Jordan realized that to get anywhere, she

Jordan sternly eyes a witness during a Judiciary Committee hearing. The freshman legislator's hard work and straightforward attitude quickly earned respect, even from conservative, segregationist colleagues: Louisiana representative John L. Rarick, for example, called her "the best congressman Texas has got."

Representative Shirley Chisholm of New York addresses a campaign rally in 1972. "I would like to have been the first [black woman in Congress]," said Jordan, "but Shirley Chisholm beat me there." In any case, added the Texas politician, "I would like to join her."

would have to catch on quickly. Of immense help would be her friend and mentor, Lyndon Johnson. The former president had begun his support of Jordan as a simple political gesture: one Texas Democrat taking care of another. But as their relationship developed, the hard-bitten, outspoken old politician had grown genuinely fond of the articulate young woman from Houston.

Neither Jordan nor other realistic freshman members of the House expected to make much of an impression during their first year in Congress. What impact newcomers do have usually depends on the committee to which they are assigned by their own party. New members are expected to request the committee of their choice and keep their fingers crossed that their requests are granted.

The 22 standing committees of the House are the means by which the legislature does most of its work:

Committees are empowered to submit new laws to the whole membership; they also consider the special areas of their concern. The Armed Services Committee, for example, deals with all legislation concerning the military; the Judiciary Committee has authority over measures relating to judicial proceedings, constitutional amendments, civil liberties, patents, and copyrights.

Because of her legal background, Jordan leaned toward the Judiciary Committee. On the other hand, the Congressional Black Caucus—an interparty group of black representatives—suggested that she ask for Armed Services. Not sure which course to pursue, Jordan turned to an old ally.

Lyndon Johnson replied to Jordan's letter with a phone call. He told her he had already pulled strings to ensure that she got the committee of her choice. She thanked him, then asked about Armed Services. The former president snorted. "You don't want to be on the Armed Services Committee," he said. "People will be cursing you from here to there, and the defense budget is always a sore spot and people don't want to spend the money."

The master politician then gave Jordan some bottom-line advice. "What you want is Judiciary," he said. "If you get the Judiciary Committee and one day someone beats hell out of you, you can be a judge."

"That made sense," reflected the congresswoman. As Johnson had promised, Jordan was assigned to the Judiciary Committee, chaired by Democrat Peter Rodino of New Jersey. She was delighted to get her first choice, although she little suspected it would soon catapult her into the national limelight.

Next came the swearing-in ceremony for new representatives. As the Texas delegation assembled, one member suggested that they surround Jordan as she took the oath of office. Another disagreed. "Well, now, but that might take away from Barbara Jordan,"

House Judiciary Committee members—who include Jordan, Elizabeth Holtzman and Charles Rangel of New York (far left and far right, respectively), and (to Jordan's right) Chairman Peter Rodino of New Jersey and committee counsel John Doar—listen to Watergate testimony in 1974.

he said. "People might not be able to tell which one she is." Jordan looked over the group of white male faces and smiled. "I think they'll be able to figure that out," she said.

Two weeks later, on January 22, Jordan received shocking news: Lyndon Johnson, 64, had died of a heart attack at his Texas ranch. Jordan and others took sad note of Johnson's death date: It was one day after his successor, Richard Nixon, had announced plans that would, in effect, do away with most of Johnson's Great Society programs, aimed at elevating the fortunes of America's blacks and other disadvantaged minorities.

From the floor of the House, freshman representative Barbara Jordan paid tribute to the nation's

36th president. "The death of Lyndon Johnson diminishes the lives of every American involved with mankind," she said in ringing tones. "Old men straightened their stooped backs because Lyndon Johnson lived; little children dared look forward to intellectual achievement because he lived; black Americans became excited about a future of opportunity, hope, justice, and dignity. Lyndon Johnson was my political mentor and my friend. I loved him and I shall miss him."

Jordan's life as a congresswoman followed a familiar pattern: A 14-hour work day, an evening spent studying the Constitution and legislative manuals, a brief night's rest, another long day's work. Physically, mentally, and emotionally, these were times that taxed her strength to the utmost. She loved every moment.

But as she had at Boston University, Jordan felt woefully ignorant and, compared to her colleagues, ill prepared to cope with the workings of national government. That she was alone in this opinion made no difference. "If there is an issue on the floor of the Congress," she said, "then I am interested in the historical background of that issue because that helps me to understand where we are now. . . . I want to be steeped in what we are discussing. I think that there are people who already know that information, but I don't. So I'm doing background for legislation all the time."

From the very beginning of Jordan's first term, Washington had been in a state of turmoil over the issue of Watergate. The scandal had begun in June 1972, when District of Columbia police arrested five men for breaking into the offices of the Democratic National Committee, quartered in the city's Watergate building. The men, who worked for President Nixon's reelection committee, had been trying to learn how much the Democrats knew about Republican campaign funds. Totally illegal, the break-in triggered an avalanche that would rock America and shatter the Nixon presidency.

Nixon assured the nation that the White House had "no involvement whatever" with the burglars, who received jail sentences in early 1973, after Nixon's landslide reelection. But rumors, then outright assertions, began to flood the capital and the press; the break-in, said informed sources, had been planned by figures high in the Nixon administration. The president, insisted these sources, had personally approved the cover-up that followed the burglary's detection.

By February 1973, the allegations had become so strong that the Senate established a committee to investigate them. Then a former White House aide revealed that Nixon had regularly taped all conversations held in his office. The Senate committee, hoping to clear up the issue of exactly what the president had known about Watergate, asked for the tapes. Nixon refused to produce them. The battle for the tapes would continue until April 1974.

Meanwhile, in October 1973, Nixon's vice-president, Spiro Agnew, resigned his office after being charged with income tax evasion.

The House Judiciary Committee was called upon to hold confirmation hearings on Nixon's choice for Agnew's replacement, Congressman Gerald Ford of Michigan.

Jordan liked Ford personally, but she considered his voting record, particularly on civil rights, a major strike against him. "I could not vote for him," she said, "because I did not feel he had the capacity to become the president" (which, as vice-president, he would if the president died or resigned).

In the end, the committee confirmed Ford; Jordan's was one of the eight votes against him. His nomination now went to the full House, where

Jordan again intended to cast a "no" vote, although she realized he would be confirmed with or without her approval. When the vote was called, however, Jordan—who almost never missed a floor vote—was absent. She was in the hospital.

Complaining of numbness in her arms and legs, she had entered the hospital for what turned out to be a week of tests. Although the tests ruled out such illnesses as cancer, the doctors could not discover the cause of Jordan's discomfort. (Since that time, she has suffered from progressively debilitating neurological impairment, about which she will not comment.)

Shortly after Agnew's resignation, Nixon ordered his attorney general, Elliot Richardson, to fire Archibald Cox, the special prosecutor Nixon himself had appointed to look into the Watergate matter. Richardson refused and resigned. The president then ordered the deputy attorney general to fire Cox. He, too, refused and resigned. Finally, acting attorney general Robert Bork wielded the hatchet; Cox left.

President Richard Nixon gestures toward transcripts of his taped White House conversations about Watergate, which he finally turned over to the House Judiciary Committee in April 1974. He had withheld the tapes for months, citing their "confidential" nature, but Jordan refused to buy the argument. "Before impeachment," she said flatly, "confidentiality falls."

This was too much for Congress. Articles of Impeachment (grounds for a trial that could lead to the president's removal from office) were introduced in the House and turned over to the Judiciary Committee for study. Mountains of testimony piled up; Barbara Jordan took it all home and spent night after night studying until daylight. "I was also reading everything I could find, from any source which had ever been written, said, or uttered about impeachment," she recalled.

Nixon had continued to withhold the "confidential" tapes, claiming "executive privilege." By this time, few believed in his innocence; all that was lacking was hard evidence—"a smoking gun"—proving that he knew about the Watergate cover-up.

Jordan, who has an almost mystical faith in constitutional government, had been hoping all

Jordan absorbs another day of Watergate hearings, a long-running event that endeared the plain-spoken Texas congress-woman to many of her fellow citizens. One family wrote her a letter saying, "We are white, Lutheran, middle class, and we must say we have been very moved, very impressed, and so happy we saw you and learned to know you on the Watergate hearings on television."

Mr. EILBERG

MS. JORDAN

along that unfolding events would somehow clear the White House. As late as 1974, she said of impeachment, "Nothing like that is going to happen. You're talking about the presidency. You're not going to impeach the president." But Nixon's determination to "stonewall" the Watergate inquiry moved her to contempt. "Before impeachment, executive privilege falls," she said firmly. "Before impeachment, confidentiality falls."

In April 1974, the White House finally released an edited transcript of some of the tapes. With them and the further damning evidence they led to, Nixon's fate was sealed. By mid-July, the Judiciary Committee prepared to conclude its study on impeachment. "It was a funny time," recalled Jordan. "Every day when we would leave those closed-door sessions the media people would chase us down the hall asking: 'Have you found the smoking gun?'"

Representatives Jordan and Rangel scan a copy of the Constitution during the Judiciary Committee's impeachment hearings. Only after intense study of the Founding Fathers' words did Jordan decide that Nixon had attempted "to subvert the Constitution" and should therefore face a trial that could lead to his removal from office. "I was not going to vote to impeach Richard Nixon [just] because I didn't like him," she said.

On July 24, Americans turned on their television sets to witness the committee's final discussion of the issue. Judiciary chairman Peter Rodino had decided that each of the committee's 35 members would have 15 minutes to make a statement. Jordan called this a waste of time. "We don't need speechmaking," she said. But few elected officials could resist 15 minutes of free, nationally broadcast, prime-time exposure. The other committee members looked at Jordan, she remarked with some amusement, as if they were thinking, "You must be out of your head."

Even by the morning of the 24th, Jordan had written no speech. She was too busy. "I was still just reading my sources and trying to be sure that I understood the charge and the offenses," she said. "I

Former New York governor Nelson Rockefeller, President Gerald Ford's nominee for the vice-presidency, tries to satisfy a quizzical Jordan during his 1974 confirmation hearings. Even such practiced and self-confident politicians as Rockefeller sometimes found Jordan's grasp of the facts and her direct gaze unnerving. "She seems to look through you," said one witness.

was not going to vote to impeach Richard Nixon [just] because I didn't like him."

Committee members spoke all day and all night; by the second evening, it was Jordan's turn. By then, she had made up her mind: "I'm going to come out for impeachment," she told her assistant. "I have decided I am going to do that, and I am going to say why." Three hours before air time, she wrote her speech. It set America on its ear.

Speaking partly from her prepared text and partly off the cuff, Jordan started out with the Constitution:

> "We the people"—it is a very eloquent beginning. But when the Constitution was completed on the 17th of September in 1787, I was not included in that "We the people." I felt for many years that somehow George Washington and Alexander Hamilton just left me out by mistake. But through the process of amendment, interpretation, and court decision, I have finally been included in "We the people."

Speaking in her usual majestic, rolling tones, Jordan went on to talk specifically of impeachment:

> Common sense would be revolted if we engaged upon this process for petty reasons. Congress has a lot to do: appropriations, tax reform, health insurance, campaign finance reform, housing, environmental protection, energy sufficiency, mass transportation. Pettiness cannot be allowed to stand in the way of such overwhelming problems. So today we are not being petty. We are trying to be big because the task we have before us is a big one.

After discussing the intentions of the Founding Fathers, Jordan quoted the words of the fourth U.S. president, James Madison: "A president is impeachable if he attempts to subvert the Constitution." Then, in a rising voice, she said:

> The Constitution charges that president with the task of taking care that the laws be faithfully executed, and yet the president has counseled his aides to commit perjury [tell lies under oath], willfully disregarded the secrecy of grand jury proceedings, concealed surreptitious entry [the Watergate burglary], attempted to compromise a federal judge while

publicly displaying his cooperation with the process of criminal justice. . . .

If the impeachment provision of the Constitution of the United States will not reach the offenses charged here, then perhaps that 18th-century Constitution should be abandoned to a 20th-century paper shredder. Has the president committed offenses and planned and directed and acquiesced in a course of conduct which the Constitution will not tolerate? That is the question. . . . We should now forthwith proceed to answer the question. It is reason and not passion which must guide our deliberations, guide our debate, and guide our decision.

When the committee clerk asked each member, "How do you vote?" on the first Article of Impeachment, Jordan responded "Aye" in a voice so soft it could barely be heard. Then she retired to a council room and cried.

The Judiciary Committee voted to impeach the president. Under normal circumstances, the full House would then vote; if it agreed with the committee, the Senate would hold a trial. How it would have turned out will never be known: On August 8, 1974, faced with almost certain disgrace and seeing no other options, Richard Nixon resigned his office. Most politically knowledgeable people, Jordan included, expected that Nixon would soon be brought to trial.

The nation had lost a president but gained a hero. "The night of the impeachment hearings," wrote Shelby Hearon, "Barbara broke through her interpreters. Thereafter, to her audience, she would be a myth of their own creating, an institution, . . . would be public property, would be a folk-hero. But on that single evening, she reached America one to one."

After the hearing, thousands of Americans called and wrote Congresswoman Jordan. The letters came from children, executives, laborers, people of all races and religions. One Houston man bought space on 25 outdoor billboards, each reading: Thank You, Barbara Jordan, for Explaining the Constitution to Us. "I

Admirers besiege Jordan for autographs at the 1977 National Women's Conference in Houston. Always a popular speaker, she has proved particularly powerful on the subject of women's rights, insisting that supporters of the Equal Rights Amendment should refuse to be deflected by "inanities and ignorance and idiots."

think you should run for President," wrote a nine-year-old boy. A secretary said, "You simply made me proud to be an American." From New England, a man wrote: "This white, Yankee Republican would be honored at some future date to campaign for our first black, first woman president—if you were the candidate."

Soon after Nixon's resignation and Gerald Ford's move to the Oval Office, Jordan's phone rang. President Ford, said the caller, would like Jordan to join Senator William Fulbright, Senator Hubert Humphrey, and a group of other distinguished lawmakers on a fact-finding trip to China. It would be a long journey but a fascinating destination. And, as Jordan said, "It's a good crowd to be traveling with." She accepted Ford's invitation.

In the middle of the trip, just after Jordan had retired to a straw mat in a remote Chinese town, a messenger knocked on her door and said she had a telephone call from the United States. She put on a robe and slippers and went out to take the call. It was from a Houston television station. "What do you think about Ford's pardon of Richard Nixon?" asked a reporter.

"What the hell are you talking about?" responded the astonished congresswoman. After finally understanding—that the new president had pardoned the old one for any crimes he "might" have committed while in office—Jordan was in shock. "I couldn't get it all together," she wrote. "Couldn't understand that the president had sent all of us as far out of the country as possible to this little province so this could happen."

Even after her return, Jordan found the pardon hard to believe. "I felt cheated," she said. "Something at least could have been resolved with the finality of a court decision, but now everything is wiped out. The country definitely got short-changed." Millions of Americans apparently agreed. In the election campaign two years later, they listened to Jordan at the Democratic convention. And at the polls, they swept Ford from office.

Meanwhile, in the 1974 Texas election, Jordan ran for a second congressional term, which she won with a staggering 84.7 percent of the vote. In the new Congress, the 94th, she was assigned to the Government Operations Committee in addition to the Judiciary Committee. She also became part of a Democratic task force commissioned to design an agenda for her party in the new Congress. And Speaker of the House Carl Albert named her one of three "at large" members of the Steering and Policy Committee of the House Democratic Caucus, making her the first black woman to so serve.

As a legislator, Jordan continued to be as fair as she knew how to be. Her impartiality sometimes evoked criticism from blacks and women, who complained that she did not always vote in their favor. Jordan was, of course, intensely interested in laws that would further the rights and interests of these groups, but she strongly believed that she had been elected as a representative of all the people, not just women and blacks.

The many bills that Jordan introduced or supported during her years in the House dealt with matters as wide-ranging as crime, civil rights, fair trade laws, federal-state revenue sharing, labor, bilingual ballots, abortion, education, and the Equal Rights Amendment (ERA). That proposed constitutional change (not yet ratified by all the necessary states) reads: "Equality of rights under the law shall not be denied or abridged by the United States or by any other state on account of sex."

Despite some complaints that she failed to show total commitment to the women's movement, Jordan took a backseat to no one in her efforts to help pass the ERA. Concluding a 1975 address at the Lyndon Baines Johnson School of Public Affairs in Austin, Texas, for example, she said:

> The women of this world—as the women of Texas, and the women of the United States of America—must exercise a leadership quality, a dedication, a concern, and a commitment which is not going to be shattered by inanities and ignorance and idiots. . . . We only want, we only ask, that when we stand up and talk about one nation under God, liberty, justice for everybody, we only want to be able to look at the flag, put our right hand over our hearts, repeat those words, and know that they are true. ◀✿▶

8

"THERE ARE NO LIMITS"

B ARBARA JORDAN SPENT six highly visible years in the U.S. House of Representatives, from 1973 until 1978. Then, at the end of her third term, she announced her retirement from public office. Most people were shocked by her decision. They felt that surely she was destined for greater things—the Senate certainly, attorney general possibly, perhaps vice-president or even president.

About her sudden move, Jordan would comment only that she needed "a new direction." After she left Washington, D.C., she became a professor at the Lyndon Baines Johnson School of Public Affairs at the University of Texas in Austin. In 1982, she accepted an appointment to the Lyndon Baines Johnson Centennial Chair in National Policy at the university. There she headed a program on national policy issues and concerns.

As a professor, Jordan treated teaching as she treated her job as a legislator—with unremitting effort, high seriousness, and thorough preparation. Her classes were crowded; the university administration decided admission to her lectures by lottery.

An obviously elated Jordan announces her retirement from public office in early 1978. Declining to elaborate on her reasons for the move, the congresswoman said only that she needed "a new direction," then headed back to Texas and a teaching post at the University of Texas.

Flooded with honors during and since serving as a U.S. congresswoman, Jordan basks in a new tribute: the 1984 renaming of Houston's main post office as the Barbara C. Jordan Building.

Jordan seemed to revel in her job as an educator. She said of her students, "I want them to be premier public servants who have a core of principles to guide them. They are my future, and the future of this country." Along with lecturing, she served as faculty adviser and counselor; every semester, she invited her students to a barbecue at her home outside Austin.

Jordan received many honors during both her political and educational careers. Among her stack of honorary degrees were diplomas from Wellesley College, Tuskegee Institute, and Southern Methodist, Tufts, and Howard universities. She also won dozens of awards: She was named Outstanding Business Woman by the Iota Lambda sorority in 1966; she received the Sojourner Truth Award from the Black Women's Development Foundation in 1974 and the Distinguished Service Award from the Texas Hospitals in 1975. In 1977, the Texas School of Health Association named Jordan a First Honorary Fellow; Phillis Wheatley High School designated her its Outstanding Graduate; and the Texas Association of Broadcasters presented her with its Distinguished Texan medal. She was elected to the Texas Women's Hall of Fame and, in 1984, was named Outstanding Woman by the American Association of University Women and—not surprisingly—Best Living Orator by the International Platform Association.

Since her 1978 retirement from politics, Jordan kept her life more private than ever. She granted almost no interviews—but then, she never was known as an easy subject for reporters. When Jordan was still in Congress, normally unflappable journalist Meg Greenfield wrote:

I can't remember being more apprehensive about an interview with a public figure than I was before (and occasionally, during) my talk with [Jordan]. The message conveyed in her every word and gesture: Don't tread on me. And she is also known for a certain brusqueness associated with another minority group to which she belongs: that of very smart people who see the point long before others have finished making it and who have a low threshold for muzzy argument or political blah.

Though Jordan continued to avoid publicity, she did make rare public-speaking appearances and performed on television as a commentator. She sometimes allowed her name to be used for certain special causes: In 1990, her signature appeared on a letter asking for contributions to the DCCC (Democratic Congressional Campaign Committee) to fight in Congress for the rights of American women.

Although Jordan moved out of the public spotlight, her oratorical skills continued to impress, and her political opinions still carried weight. She aired some of them in 1987, when President Ronald Reagan tried to fill a Supreme Court vacancy by nominating archconservative Judge Robert H. Bork. The nomination of Bork—the man who, as acting attorney general, had carried out President Nixon's order to fire special Watergate prosecutor Archibald Cox—outraged many liberals, including Jordan.

Jordan felt so strongly about Bork, in fact, that she not only testified against him before the Senate Judiciary Committee; she even made one of her increasingly rare television appearances. In an October 1987 broadcast of "Meet the Press," an interviewer asked Jordan what the liberals would gain if they succeeded in blocking Bork's nomination.

"What will be gained," replied Jordan, "is the absence of a voice on the Supreme Court which would threaten to reverse centuries-long, publicly held policy positions which this country is comfortable with. Judge Bork is the kind of voice that would see threatened those rights which everyone has become so familiar and so comfortable with and

Speaking from a wheelchair, Jordan seconds the nomination of a fellow Texan, Lloyd Bentsen, as the Democratic candidate for vice-president in July 1988. "If we rely on reason as our guide," she said in her convention speech, "reason will help us to do the right things."

which are so important to the individual." (Bork failed to win Senate confirmation for the Court seat, later filled by Judge Anthony Kennedy of California.) Not long after Bork's defeat, Jordan made another nationally televised appearance, this one at the 1988 Democratic National Convention. Jordan took the podium to second the nomination of a Texas colleague, Senator Lloyd Bentsen, as the running mate of presidential candidate Michael Dukakis of Massachusetts. The Democrats would go on to lose the election to Republicans George Bush and Dan Quayle, but not because Jordan failed to ignite a convention with another riveting speech. On this occasion, she emphasized the Democrats' need for unity and reason:

> You know, the people who founded America were very smart. Those founders warned us not to become overcome by factions, but to rely on reason as our guide. If we rely on reason as our guide, reason will temper and tenure our emotions. Reason will help us to do the right things. Reason will tutor us toward saying the right things.

In August 1988, shortly after the convention, bulletins flashed across the country: Barbara Jordan, 52, had been found unconscious and floating facedown in the swimming pool of her Austin, Texas, home. Rushed to a nearby hospital, Jordan was revived by a team of doctors who later announced that the former U.S. representative had narrowly missed—by "5 minutes, 10 minutes at most"—suffering severe brain damage and possible death.

Jordan never explained the near-fatal accident, but to the relief of friends and fans she recuperated from the ordeal quickly. Wire services soon carried photographs that showed her in a hospital bed, smiling and giving the hand sign (raised first and fourth fingers, folded thumb and middle fingers) of the Longhorns, the University of Texas's football team. Reporters noted that although she was some-

Beaming after her recovery from an almost fatal swimming-pool accident in August 1988, Jordan leaves an Austin hospital to return to the University of Texas. The congresswoman-turned-college professor made no secret of her concern for her students: "I want them to be premier public servants who have a core of principles to guide them," she said. "They are my future, and the future of the country."

what secretive about her personal life, Jordan had never concealed her passion for football, especially as played by Texas teams.

Jordan died from viral pneumonia as a complication of leukemia on January 17, 1996, in her home state of Texas.

Who was Barbara Jordan? She detested being called a symbol, but time and circumstances have made her just that. She symbolized the achievements of three groups long discriminated against in America: blacks, women, and southerners. To employ another word Jordan would probably scorn, she was also a workaholic. Always striving to master whatever job she had taken on, she was known for intense, almost religious dedication to her work.

An unsentimental but acute journalist once called Jordan "as cozy as a pile driver, though considerably more impressive." And a 1975 *Wall Street Journal* profile noted that her terms in Congress had earned her "more honor and perhaps more power than most members . . . can look forward to in a lifetime."

Jordan, who was observed dancing the "bump" at Washington gatherings, enjoyed good times with her friends. She also maintained a close, warm relationship with her family. Her sister Rose Mary says that they communicated on a weekly basis: "We visit her and she comes home to Houston, too."

But Jordan was also reclusive. Sometimes described as "cold" and "aloof," she could be bitingly sarcastic. According to fellow Texas representative Charles Wilson, "Barbara doesn't try to play possum on you; she doesn't mind letting you know that she's got a very, very high I.Q."

On the other hand, continued Wilson, Jordan "doesn't embarrass you by making you feel that you're nowhere close to being as smart as she is. It's an amazing thing how she can be standing there schooling you about something and still make you feel that you knew all that right along. Not all smart people can do that; some of them love to make you feel right ignorant."

An unabashed Jordan admirer, Wilson struggled to find words that would accurately describe her. "It's that along with her superior intelligence and legislative skill," he said, "she also has a certain *moral authority* and a—it's just presence, and it all comes together in a way that sort of grabs you."

Why did Jordan, not yet at the height of what seemed a brilliant political career, leave public office so abruptly? Had she become disenchanted with the slow, sometimes devious workings of government? Was it her deteriorating health? Did she truly wish to strike out in a new direction? No one, except for those really close to her, can answer those questions. And they will not do so in public.

Despite her years of outstanding service in the academic field, many people expressed the belief, or perhaps merely the wish, that Jordan would return to public life in some capacity. She is too inspiring a figure, too commanding a presence, they said, not to remain a political leader.

Jordan steadfastly refused to comment on her future plans. In 1981 she remarked, "I don't deal with *ever*. I deal with now." And *now* for her meant helping young Americans fulfill their roles in their nation's destiny, a subject about which she would speak at length and with undisguised passion. In a 1989 interview with photojournalist Brian Lanker (included in his book *I Dream a World: Portraits of Black Women Who Changed America*), Jordan talked about being black and being young:

> I am telling the young people that if you're dissatisfied . . . with the way things are, then you have got to resolve to change them. . . . It is a burden of black people that we have to do more than talk. We have somehow got to sacrifice our

Speaking with characteristic gusto, Jordan addresses a 1989 union convention in California. "Black people," asserts the much-acclaimed speaker, "have to do more than talk. We have somehow to sacrifice our lives as an example to move young people along." Perhaps, she says hopefully, "something in my life will help move a young person...to stay in school."

lives as an example to move young people along so that they will understand that it is a long, slow, tough road to really make it so that it lasts. I have got to offer myself as a role model to others so that perhaps something in my life will help move a young black person who might otherwise drop out to stay in school. That is part of my mission.

Finally, in a poetic tribute to her native state and to the human spirit, Jordan said:

It may not be polished, may not be smooth, and it may not be silky, but it is there. I believe that I get from the soil and the spirit of Texas the feeling that I, as an individual, can accomplish whatever I want to and that there are no limits, that you can just keep going, just keep soaring. I like that spirit. ❧

CHRONOLOGY

—— ✤ ——

1936   Born Barbara Charline Jordan on February 21 in Houston, Texas

1952   Graduates from Phillis Wheatley High School; wins National United Ushers Association Oratorical Contest

1956   Graduates magna cum laude from Texas Southern University

1959   Graduates from Boston University Law School

1962   Runs for the Texas House of Representatives; loses election

1964   Loses second campaign for the Texas legislature

1966   Elected to the Texas State Senate, becoming the state's first black senator since 1883; gains support of President Lyndon B. Johnson

1968   Wins second term in Texas senate

1972   Serves as Texas governor for a day, becoming first black woman to head any American state government; elected to U.S. House of Representatives; assigned to House Judiciary Committee

1973   Begins to suffer from neurological impairment that will eventually confine her to a wheelchair

1974   Gains national recognition with televised speech during impeachment hearings on President Richard M. Nixon; elected to second term in Congress

1976   Delivers keynote speech at Democratic National Convention; wins third congressional term

1979   Retires from public life; becomes professor at University of Texas

1982   Appointed to LBJ Centennial Chair in National Policy at University of Texas

1987   Testifies against confirmation of Robert H. Bork to U.S. Supreme Court

1988   Seconds nomination of vice-presidential candidate Lloyd Bentsen at Democratic National Convention; recovers from near-fatal swimming pool accident

1992   Continues to lecture and teach public affairs at University of Texas

1996   Dies in Texas on January 17 from viral pneumonia as a complication of leukemia

FURTHER READING

————— ·❦· —————

Archer, Jules. *The Incredible Sixties*. San Diego: Harcourt Brace Jovanovich, 1986.

Chamberlain, Hope. *A Minority of Members: Women in the United States Congress*. New York: Praeger, 1973.

Drew, Elizabeth. *Washington Journal: The Events of 1973–1974*. New York: Macmillan, 1984.

Falkof, Lucille. *Lyndon B. Johnson: 36th President of the United States*. New York: Garrett, 1989.

Haskins, James. *Barbara Jordan*. New York: Dial Press, 1977.

Haskins, James and Kathleen Brenner. *The 60s Reader*. New York: Viking Press, 1988.

Jordan, Barbara, and Shelby Hearon. *Barbara Jordan: A Self-Portrait*. New York: Doubleday, 1979.

Kosof, Anna. *The Civil Rights Movement and Its Legacy*. New York: Watts, 1989.

Manchester, William. *The Glory and the Dream: A Narrative History of America, 1932–1972*. Boston: Little, Brown, 1974.

Staff of the Washington Post. *The Fall of a President*. New York: Dell, 1974.

Strachtman, Tom. *Decade of Shocks: Dallas to Watergate 1963–1974*. New York: Simon & Schuster, 1983.

INDEX

PICTURE CREDITS

ROSE BLUE is the author of nearly two dozen books for children and young adults, including *Cold Rain on the Water*, which was selected by the National Council for the Social Studies and the Children's Book Council as one of the notable 1979 children's trade books in the field of social studies. Two of her books, *Grandma Didn't Wave Back* (1972) and *My Mother the Witch* (1980), were adapted for television and aired on NBC-TV as young people's specials.

CORINNE NADEN is the author of 15 books for children and young adults, including *Ronald McNair* in Chelsea House's BLACK AMERICANS OF ACHIEVEMENT SERIES, and coauthor of 3 books for children's librarians and teachers. A former children's book editor, she served four years in the U.S. Navy, editing a weekly newspaper and writing training-film scripts. She is a graduate of New York University.

NATHAN IRVIN HUGGINS, one of America's leading scholars in the field of black studies, helped select the titles for the BLACK AMERICANS OF ACHIEVEMENT SERIES, for which he also served as senior consulting editor. He was the W.E.B. Du Bois Professor of History and of Afro-American Studies at Harvard University and its director of the W.E.B. Du Bois Institute for Afro-American Research. He received his doctorate from Harvard in 1962 and returned there as a professor in 1980 after teaching at Columbia University, the University of Massachusetts, Lake Forest College, and the California State College at Long Beach. He was the author of four books and dozens of articles, including *Black Odyssey: The Afro-American Ordeal in Slavery*, *The Harlem Renaissance*, and *Slave and Citizen: The Life of Frederick Douglass*, and was associated with the Children's Television Workshop, National Public Radio, the Boston Athenaeum, the Museum of Afro-American History, the Howard Thurman Educational Trust, and Upward Bound. Professor Huggins died in 1989, at the age of 62, in Cambridge, Massachusetts.